Praise for *A Chinese*

John Jung is a phenomenon: a career academic turned "outsider" scholar to reshape our understanding of the Chinese American experience by his novel historical studies, especially of communities in his native South. *A Chinese American Odyssey* provides readers yet another work to savor. Part memoir, part how-to book, it provides a detailed and engaging study of author Jung's transformation from a psychologist into a historian, as well as lessons for independent researchers.

Greg Robinson, Professor of History, University of Quebec. *After Camp: Portraits in Midcentury Japanese American Life and Politics*

A Chinese American Odyssey documents John Jung's fascinating metamorphosis as he retired from psychology to become an important voice in Chinese American history. And John's richly contextualized tales of his unique experiences as a Chinese makes the book an insightful cultural biography. Anyone interested in Chinese America, or how to succeed in a post-retirement career, should read this highly enjoyable memoir.

Yong Chen, Professor of History, University of California, Irvine. *Chop Suey USA: The Story of Chinese Food in America.*

A fascinating book about a retirement journey that started with the author's memoir about growing up in a laundry in Macon, Georgia, where his family were the only Chinese. He next published three more rich and important books about Chinese immigrants in North America. *A Chinese American Odyssey* is an account of a vital retirement, of people he met along the way, history of Chinese in North America, the ins and outs of self-publishing, the book talk circuit, and much more.

Paul Rosenblatt, Professor Emeritus, Family Social Science, University of Minnesota. *The Impact of Racism on African American Families: Literature as Social Science*

With a researcher's reliance on evidence, a painter's eye for detail, and a comedian's well-timed punch lines, John Jung's four previous narratives have shown how to write well, live well, and merge the two in mindful social contemplation. He has a keen sense of style and craft, which I witnessed as a student in his research classes where his commitment to train up-and-coming scholars was infectious. *Odyssey* clearly shows he is a master teacher. Jung's books epitomize good scholarship: his writing informs and compels us to want more beauty and time for reflection. His studies of the Chinese American experience in a Southern context humanize us all by complicating the South we think we know. *Odyssey* focuses on the *process* of writing life stories to open the curtain to reveal the awful beauty of the personal difficulties that have made his Chinese American histories so impactful with an ever-growing regional, national, and international audience. Dr. Jung demonstrates the intellectual power of creative scholarship and his generous spirit offers practical guidance for those who want to move ahead with telling their own story.

Stephanie Y. Evans, Chair, African American Studies, Africana Women's Studies, and History, Clark Atlanta University *Black Women in the Ivory Tower, 1850-1954: An Intellectual History.*

John Jung has done it again with his quirky memoir "A Chinese American Odyssey." He provides a wonderfully kaleidoscopic view of Chinese American history from inside out and outside in and this time he has even thrown in the kitchen sink in this accounting of his incredible, post-academia publishing career. All will be the richer for reading this lively tale. Tag along on his varied adventures, many of a serendipitous nature, in search of some fast fading history and those who lived it, including himself.

Mel Brown, *Chinese Heart of Texas: The San Antonio Community 1875-1975. TexAsia; San Antonio's Asian Communities 1978-2008.*

John Jung is the epitome of a retiree who never fades away. He just changed his academic focus to expand his horizons into the field of Chinese American social history, and expose the struggles and triumphs of the second and third generations of laundry operators and restaurateurs who planted footholds in many a Chinatown.

Sylvia Sun Minnick, *SAMFOW: The San Joaquin Chinese Legacy.*

A

CHINESE AMERICAN

ODYSSEY

How a Retired Psychologist

Makes a Hit as a Historian

John Jung

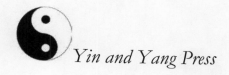*Yin and Yang Press*

LCCN: 2014916300
ISBN-13: 978-1502473653
ISBN-10: 1502473658

A Chinese American Odyssey
/John Jung

p. cm.
Includes bibliographical references.

Yin & Yang Press

To Those Who Had to Eat Bitterness

So Their Descendants Could Taste Sweetness

Table of Contents

Foreword

John Jung never aspired to be astonishing. It just keeps happening. After a long, productive career as a psychology professor and researcher, he started a whole new career. Like Odysseus retiring from war to become an intrepid traveler, in retirement John began an odyssey of astonishing creativity and growth.

His journey began with a memoir, but not the sort expected of a retired psychology professor. He pivoted to a new topic and genre. A flavor of his first post-retirement book, *Southern Fried Rice*, is reflected by a reviewer's comments printed on the back cover:

"... Based on his experience as a child in the only Chinese family in [1930s] Macon, Georgia . . . Jung's story is a fascinating account of the negotiation of personal and ethnic identity in a foreign environment. His narrative highlights many of the features of the larger society, including both government policy and situational practice that shape the lives of immigrants, both then and now."

Including this new book, "A Chinese American Odyssey," John, the astonisher, has published five books as a public historian of the Chinese in America. Astonishing. Again.

Perhaps his talent for astonishment emerged when he and his family lived above their laundry from the 1920s until the mid-1950s, the only Chinese in the city. Operating a laundry was not unusual for an immigrant Chinese family, but its location was: the harshly segregated, Deep South city of Macon, Georgia.

There were only two social addresses in 1930s Macon: White or Black. The Jung children posed a dilemma for practitioners of racial apartheid. Apparently the local cultural solution was declaring John and his family white or at least treating them as non-black. He remembers as a small boy being scolded by a white woman for drinking from a water fountain reserved for blacks. He had been socially declared white, but his mother taught it wasn't true. He was Chinese. But he was still directed to the white water fountains and attended the white-only public schools.

He didn't feel Chinese no matter what his mother told him, or racist insults assumed. He did not know Chinese cultural ways of being and interacting, something he quickly discovered when teenaged John, his mother, and siblings moved into San Francisco's large, robust Chinese community. He was accepted as Chinese, but he never identified fully with being Chinese.

In high school, college, and graduate school, John practiced cultural assimilation. Armed with a Ph.D. from Northwestern's prestigious psychology department, and mentored by a leading learning researcher of the era (B. J. Underwood), John succeeded as a professor in Canada and California. He taught well, published often, and did not perish.

Many who knew John from graduate school to retirement (including myself) never learned of his family history. He never talked about it. To my knowledge he never expressed any strong interest in racial and ethnic topics or issues, even during '60s and '70s when they were often headline news. So he is accurate when he reports in this book that becoming a public historian of Chinese in America was "especially improbable because my personal identification as a Chinese American was not a strong one, partly because my contact with Chinese people had been minimal during most of my life, especially in my youth.... During my high school and college years, although I developed cordial friendships with Chinese peers in a Chinatown community center and church, I always felt I was not "as Chinese" as they were. .... my Chinese identity that had started to develop during my high school and college years in the San Francisco Bay area deteriorated, and continued to be minimal at best for many years."

Given this history, neither John, or any of us who knew him the last 55 years, would have predicted in retirement he'd become a significant contributor to Chinese American history studies and a compelling voice for Chinese Americans growing up in families that operated laundries, groceries, and restaurants.

But there's more to John's post-retirement books than interesting history and sound scholarship. In retirement, the books he's written recount a personal journey from fully assimilated American to discovery of a Chinese identity to a fully bicultural Chinese American identity. In a sense, this book might be titled

"An American Chinese Odyssey" to reflect better the direction taken in his post-retirement journey.

Personal growth is also an underlying theme in Homer's *The Odyssey*. Growth portrayed as a journey of challenging times, multiple temptations, and successes too. "A Chinese American Odyssey" recounts John's growth not only in a new discipline. but in his feeling Chinese.

But this book is much more than a story of his personal growth. It proves that retirement need not be an end, but can be a beginning. It's an inspiration not only for old professors, but everyone — because sooner or later, if you are lucky, you will retire and wonder what's left. A lot is possible, if you know John's story.

For those inspired in retirement to become an author, "A Chinese American Odyssey" can help. In this book John focused "on the creative process of research, discovery, and writing, the self-publishing process, and the tasks of self-promotion and marketing." Describing the book, he writes, "This is a personal account, and not a "How To" guide. Rather I describe the ups and downs of planned and unplanned experiences that unfolded in my new career."

"A Chinese American Odyssey" implies in several places that John regards this as his final act as public historian. But knowing his history, who would be astonished if he did it again — started a new research project, wrote another book? I wouldn't. After all, Odysseus didn't remain idle when he ended his journey.

Ronald Gallimore
Distinguished Professor Emeritus
University of California, Los Angeles

Preface

After more than 40 years as a professor of psychology, I retired in 2007 and stumbled into a new career in which I studied the lives and experiences of Chinese immigrants and their descendants in the U. S. and Canada in small businesses such as laundries, restaurants, and grocery stores. I wrote four books that documented their struggles to survive in an unfamiliar land against staunch racial prejudice and overwhelming hardships. I also publicized my findings at over 80 book signing events across the country.

The present book is quite different in its purpose from my previous four books, and I will not refer to the content from those books except in passing. Instead, the focus of this book is on the creative process of researching and writing, and on the self-publishing process, and the tasks of self-promotion and marketing. This is a personal account, and not a "How To" guide. But anyone researching, writing, and promoting a book on *any* subject may be able to learn from the ups and downs of planned and unplanned experiences that unfolded in my new career. In this book I will describe some of the most significant events, people, and experiences associated with my post-retirement career as a public historian.

With *A Chinese American Odyssey* I hope that seeing how I studied, wrote, and spoke about the history of Chinese in America will help guide and encourage others to undertake similar writing and publishing activities to further the understanding and improvement of the place of Chinese in America. What I have learned may help others avoid some of my mistakes and obstacles that confronted me.

This book, like chop suey, is a mixture of ingredients, and multifaceted. It includes topics of history as well as pragmatic issues, such as how I researched, wrote, published, and promoted books without a traditional publisher. The playing field for publishing has not only been leveled, it has been revolutionized. The availability of many software tools for authors, many free or inexpensive, and the existence of rich sources of archival material on the Web has redefined the process and means of writing books. For example, the inclusion of hyperlinks in the e-book version of this book allows readers to access much more information than is presented in this book by simply clicking on the links. Since hyperlinks in a paperback book are *not* active or functional, I have supplied them as endnotes for each chapter, which unfortunately, is not an ideal solution because readers will have the tedious task of typing hyperlinks accurately into the *URL* window of a Web browser to access the additional material. To spare paperback readers from this arduous task, I placed all links in the book on a website: http://chineseamericanodyssey.webs.com/links.

My journey has been exciting because of many unexpected experiences and accidental discoveries, evidence that even the best of plans change over the course of research. Many of the lessons I learned should be of interest and value to aspiring nonfiction writers on many other topics who may not know what lies ahead for them.

Without the encouragement, advice, and support of many friends, family, and colleagues, I would not have managed to take this journey. I owe special thanks to historians Xiaolan Bao, Sylvia Sun Minnick, Judy Yung, Mel Brown, Greg Robinson, and Yong Chen and to psychologists Ronald Gallimore, Rod Wong, Paul Rosenblatt, Stanley Sue, and Kay Deaux. Thanks to Phyllis for her patience and indulgence in supporting my many hours spent on this odyssey, at home and on the road.

The expert editorial guidance of Mike Revzin and Marina Bang greatly improved the readability and clarity of the book. I am also appreciative of the graphic skills and artistic talent of Marina Bang who gave generously of her time in the creation and development of the compelling book cover.

JJ
Cypress, California
November 2014

1 The Journey Begins

A journey of a thousand miles begins with a single step.
Lao Tzu (604 BC - 531 BC)

To say that my life after retiring from more than 40 years as a professor of psychology has been a surprise to me is an understatement. Until retirement I had never considered researching, let alone, writing about the history of Chinese in America.

My new venture was especially improbable because my personal identification as a Chinese American was not a strong one, partly because my contact with Chinese people had been minimal during most of my life, especially in my youth. Our family was the only Chinese one in the entire city of Macon, Georgia, where my immigrant parents from China came in the 1920s and earned a living running a laundry until the early 1950s.

Growing up under such extreme cultural isolation in a time and place when Jim Crow segregation[1] was still unchallenged in the Deep South, I first experienced uncertainty, then confusion, and eventually conflict in thinking about myself as a Chinese. At a superficial level, I knew I was *Chinese* because my immigrant parents were not fluent in English so my first language was Chinese. My mother reminded me incessantly that we were Chinese, and not the same as whites. She was doubtless motivated by a concern to prepare us for prejudicial treatment we could expect to receive from whites and blacks. She formed such expectations from her own experience receiving racial taunts such as "Chinese eat rats" from children on the street. Even if she never mentioned it, since everyone else in Macon was either white or black, I was quite aware that we were different or in other words, Chinese. Growing up in this situation, we were often treated as exotic or at least foreign.

Mother was especially bitter about the immigration barriers to Chinese imposed by exclusionary laws against Chinese, which were in place in one form or another from the mid-1800s to 1965. She told us that she and my father, like many other Chinese immigrants, had to resort to purchasing false papers to gain entry to the United States. I felt conflicted knowing that due to the unfair laws against Chinese, my parents had circumvented this barrier by using false identities. She also described the physical and mental ordeal that she suffered when detained and interrogated at Angel Island in San Francisco Bay - the West Coast equivalent of Ellis Island - when she immigrated in 1928. I was shocked to learn of this mistreatment of Chinese immigrants and I was upset and angry about what my parents had experienced. These discoveries made me reluctant at times to want to think of myself as Chinese.

Jung family, 1946: Mary, John, mother Grace, Eugenia, father Frank, George.

When my two sisters, brother, and I approached our adolescent years, my parents began to plan for our future, which they felt was not good for us in the South. In the late 1940s, they decided it was time to move the family, in stages, to San Francisco, where we could escape our cultural isolation. They felt their children would become more "Chinese" once we were living in a Chinese community.

I recall being reluctant to leave Macon, because it was the only place I had lived in and I could not imagine what it would be like to live in a large city clear across the country. Once we arrived in San Francisco, or *Dai Fow* (Big City) as Chinese called it because of its large Chinese community, I found my new life to be exciting and challenging. Overnight, we went from being the only Chinese in town to being just one of thousands – and many adjustments had to be made.

Talk about culture shock! Coming from Georgia and foods such as southern fried chicken, black-eyed peas, grits, and corn bread, what was I to make of egg rolls, chow mein, won ton, dim sum, tofu, and bird's nest soup - none of which I had ever tasted in Macon where the only place I could get Chinese food was from my mother's wok. I was similarly unacquainted with many other aspects of Chinese customs and traditions such as yin and yang, Chinese New Year parades, kung fu, tai chi, feng shui, and mahjong. I had a lot to learn about being Chinese.

I was curious and interested to meet other Chinese of my age. I soon had cordial and friendly interactions with my numerous newfound Chinese American peers in San Francisco, but it did not take long for me to conclude that I was not as *Chinese* as they were. I did not immediately embrace being Chinese. I was not familiar with most Chinese customs and attitudes. I was an outsider to the Chinese community whereas my Chinese American peers had all grown up with social networks consisting almost entirely of other Chinese. My limited ability to speak and understand Chinese also made me uncomfortable.

It seemed to me that my Chinese schoolmates preferred to hang out only with cliques of other Chinese, and avoided socializing with non-Chinese. This separation was probably due in part to the longstanding racial barriers in California between Chinese and whites, which still existed to some extent. I found this low social contact of Chinese with whites somewhat abnormal at first because after all, I had attended all-white schools in Georgia. But in San Francisco, I soon fell in line with the norms and I socialized mostly with other Chinese at school and made little effort to mingle with non-Chinese students.

During my high school and college years, although I developed cordial friendships with Chinese peers in a historic

Chinatown community center, Cameron House,[2] and the First Presbyterian Chinese Church, I always felt I was not "as Chinese" as they were. After finishing my undergraduate college studies, my contact with Chinese people soon declined drastically. I left San Francisco to attend graduate school at Northwestern University in Evanston, a well-to-do predominately white suburb of Chicago with a student body that was mainly white. After completing my Ph.D. studies, I continued to find myself in a mostly white world as I taught psychology for several decades at Long Beach State, with three years at York University in Toronto, sandwiched in during the mid-1960s. During most of these years there were few Chinese students, other than international students, at either university. Consequently, my Chinese identity that had started to develop during my high school and college years in the San Francisco Bay Area deteriorated, and continued to be minimal at best for many years.

By the time I was 30, and yet unmarried with no prospects in view, I felt parental pressure. A major reason for not marrying was the expectation that I would marry a Chinese. I understood why my parents felt this way, and I did not object, but the reality was that I did not have much opportunity to meet and date Chinese women. Furthermore, the demands of my academic career became my primary concern, further limiting my time and effort to search for a prospective Chinese bride.

Like many children of Chinese, as well as other immigrants, I was conflicted between embracing the culture of my parents and that of mainstream white America. Wanting to fit in and assimilate with the dominant culture, I questioned, or even rejected, some of the values and customs of my immigrant parents. The prejudices and discriminatory barriers against Chinese by white America generated my feelings of inferiority as someone of Chinese descent. Sometimes I experienced embarrassment, and at other times resentment, over being "different." These reactions made me feel victimized. Why me? Why did I have to be a child of immigrants? Why did I have to be Chinese? Well, not as Chinese as my parents, but I did not want to be even Chinese-American. In that era, children of immigrants were labeled as "hyphenated-Americans" Although blatant anti-Chinese feelings have diminished over recent decades, my ambivalence, if not outright rejection of a Chinese identify when I was growing up stemmed from society's bias in favor of white America. Accounts of American history, until the civil rights activism of the late 1960s, had been for the most part a history of white American men. The place of Chinese, as well as other Asian immigrants, had been largely ignored. Inclusion of coverage of the contributions and achievements of Chinese to American society would have helped instill in me a greater acceptance of my Chinese self.

Around 2005, as I was preparing to retire from a long academic career as a psychologist who taught and researched the psychology of alcohol use, I began to think about writing a memoir about our family experiences living in Georgia as the only Chinese in our town for many years before we moved to San Francisco to be in a Chinese community. As a young adult, I never thought this story would be of much interest, even though over the years many acquaintances had expressed surprise, curiosity, and interest in learning more about what life was like for us in Georgia and subsequently in San Francisco. However, being someone who is a private person, I was not comfortable with the thought of making our family story public. I also had real doubts whether I could write such a book, which called for a different mindset and skills from those I used in writing psychology textbooks.

My memoir, *Southern Fried Rice: Life in A Chinese Laundry in the Deep South*, fortunately was well received. Writing the book gave me personal satisfaction in paying tribute to my parents for enduring their lives of hardship and isolation in the South. They did not live to know about the book; indeed, I know I could not have written it while they were alive because they would have objected strenuously. During the process of researching and writing it, I discovered so much information about the difficult lives of other Chinese who had run laundries throughout North America that I felt the urge to write another book to honor them -- *Chinese Laundries: Tickets to Survival on Gold Mountain*.

Writing these two books about the lives of Chinese laundrymen and their families led me down a new path as I received, quite by chance, several opportunities to speak across the country. These events allowed me to meet many Chinese who either had owned or worked in laundries, knew someone who had a laundry, or grew up and worked in a family-run laundry. These experiences were transformative for me as they generated my motivation to learn more about the history of Chinese in America that I had never been taught. One thing led to another, and before I realized it, I had written four books on the Chinese experience in North America and at last count given over 80 talks at venues that included Chinese American historical museums, Chinese community organizations, academic conferences, public libraries, Chinese churches, literary conferences, bookstores, retirement communities, and even a fifth grade class.

In short, my retirement led to a new career - one that taught me the importance and power of studying history. During the course of this endeavor, I have had many remarkable experiences, many of which were quite unexpected or unplanned. The goal of this book is to provide a detailed journal of the events and people involved in my adventure and to analyze the significance of my work for myself as well as for my readers and audiences, Chinese as well as non-Chinese.

In this book I will describe my excursion into uncharted terrain, one that included many surprising encounters, fortuitous breaks, support and mentoring from new networks, inspired actions, calculated risks, some disappointments, frequent doubts, positive responses from many readers and audiences, and plenty of old-fashioned hard work and determination.

Mentor and friend, historian Xiaolan Bao

I did not realize it at the time, but before I wrote a single word about growing up in the South, the late Xiaolan Bao, my friend and a professor of history at California State University, Long Beach, had encouraged me by persuading me that my story was an important one to document and share. As an expression of friendship, when it was published, she gave me an autographed copy of her scholarly masterpiece, *Holding Up More than Half The Sky: Chinese Women Garment Workers in New York City, 1948-92.* [3]

In 2005, she suggested that I submit a proposal to speak about my life growing up in Georgia at a forthcoming Chinese American history conference in San Francisco. I felt very insecure about speaking to an audience of historians, but she calmly reassured me that my topic was of interest and that I would do well.

Given such affirmation by an accomplished scholar, I forged ahead and got my feet wet in Asian American studies, a move that I have never regretted. Unfortunately, Xiaolan died of cancer just before the conference and never got to see the finished book that she helped launch.

Xiaolan Bao, colleague and mentor at California State University, Long Beach

Lulu, a print-on-demand pioneer

The traditional way to publish a book involves a difficult and slow process. You have to find a publishing company, usually possible only with a literary agent who reviews and assesses the market potential of your book. However, even finding an agent to represent a new author is not easy. If you do succeed in getting an agent who sees promise, he or she will try to market the book to a publisher. Once a contract is offered and accepted, your manuscript undergoes extensive review and editing. Next, the publisher develops the book design, layout, and format. Then the publisher promotes and distributes your book to bookstores, and elsewhere. The entire process is daunting, and it might be well over a year between your completion of the manuscript and it being published as a book. The process is difficult and time-consuming, and the odds of success are low.

Fortunately for me, around 2000, a revolution in the book publishing industry was occurring with the development of new computer technology variously known as print-on-demand (POD) or self-publishing. Authors no longer have to go the traditional route, but can, in varying degrees, take a "do it yourself" route, and publish a book within a few weeks or months at very minimal or almost no cost. One major reason for the financial viability of this new approach is that copies are not printed until orders are received. No longer will there be inventories of thousands of copies that might never be sold, stored in garages or warehouses.

One of the early print-on-demand leaders, Lulu.com, was attractive to me because the upfront financial costs were minimal, an important consideration since I really had no idea about how many copies I could sell. In contrast, traditional publishers decide in advance, based on market analyses, a specified number of orders – and an inventory is created that may result in many unsold books.

Given my doubts about the potential of a memoir about Chinese in the South, I was reluctant to spend much money to find out whether I was correct. Using Lulu.com as my printer, all I needed to spend was time, effort, and incidental amounts for paper, printer toner, and postage. I decided I would create the book myself from start to finish and do the writing, editing, formatting, promoting, and selling myself.

The availability of this method for self-publishing was encouraging because I did not think that I would be able to attract the interest of a traditional publisher. I thought, rightly or wrongly, that my subject would not have a large market, and hence, be unlikely to be profitable for a publisher. I did approach two university presses with a book prospectus, thinking that the value of the book might be more important to them than financial considerations. I was wrong. One university press actually wrote that their editors found the story compelling but their market research suggested that they would not sell enough copies to be profitable.

While I was disappointed with the criteria they used for their decision, I could understand their position from a financial perspective. However, their decision to let the balance sheet prevail over historic value only made me more determined because I wanted to prove that their assessment of the potential market was wrong.

I decided to self-publish the book with Lulu.com, but the idea of having a name like "lulu" as my publisher did not seem suitable for a book on Chinese American history. It seemed somewhat frivolous to me, so I decided instead to devise my own publisher name. My choice, *Yin and Yang Press*, felt ideal for a book on Chinese American history. To my delight and surprise, no other publisher had taken this name.

Time has proved I was right in my appraisal of the potential of the story of our family's life in Georgia, as *Southern Fried Rice* has led to many compliments from readers and book talk audiences - and good sales. A recent reader went so far as to say that she hated to see the book come to an end!

Endnotes

[1] Jim Crow, a minstrel character, came to represent the oppressive racial conditions for blacks in the American South from the Reconstruction period right after the Civil War. http://www.ferris.edu/jimcrow/what.htm

[2] http://www.cameronhouse.org/aboutUs/history.html

[3] Xiaolan Bao. *Holding Up More than Half The Sky: Chinese Women Garment Workers in New York City, 1948-92.* Urbana, IL.: University of Illinois Press, 2006.

2 Southern Fried Rice

More than half a century after my parents moved our family to San Francisco, I embarked on the task of writing a memoir about our family's life in Macon and, after some false starts, my work eventually came to life. As my mother's ability to survive her difficult life situation was a central theme in the memoir, and her American name was Grace, it seemed fitting to use as its title, *Amazing Grace*. After much deliberation, that choice was abandoned because the strong association to the song of that name might suggest that my mother was deeply religious or spiritual, which she was not.

I decided to search for a term that would clearly be tied with the South and, in a moment of last-minute inspiration, I thought, "southern fried." Thus, my title became *Southern Fried Rice*, followed by a subtitle, *Life in A Chinese Laundry in the Deep South*. It proved to be an excellent choice, as any reference to "Southern Fried" guaranteed an association with the region, and "fried rice" is strongly connected with Chinese due to this popular type of dish served in Chinese American restaurants. The title, of course, is not entirely accurate because we ran a laundry, not a restaurant, but so far only one person has quibbled about that flaw in the title.

Background of Chinese in Macon

During the years when I was living in Macon, I had never wondered if there had been other Chinese living there before my parents arrived in 1928. If I had actually thought about it, I should have assumed there had been at least one Chinese laundryman in Macon before them and that my father bought the laundry from him. It would have been more unlikely for my parents to open a laundry in a town where none existed than for them to find a town where an established laundry was for sale, perhaps by an older Chinese who was retiring.

It was only after we moved to San Francisco when I was 15 that I got the idea that there had in fact been Chinese in Macon long before my parents came there. When my father left Macon for good in 1956, the local newspaper printed a "farewell and best wishes" column to acknowledge his departure, salute him for being a good member of the community, and wish him well in San Francisco. The headline, *Not A Chinese in Our Town For First Time in A Century,* surprised me when I saw it but at the time I was too young to pay much attention to it.[1]

Macon had Chinese laundries as early as 1885

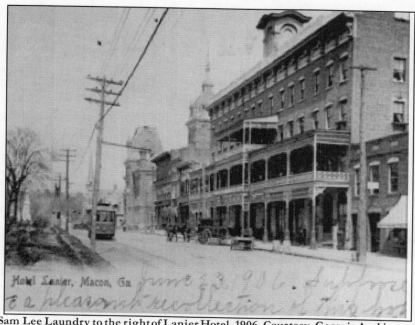

Sam Lee Laundry to the right of Lanier Hotel, 1906. Courtesy, Georgia Archives.

Five decades later, as I researched Macon's history in 2005, the recollection of that article's headline prompted me to contact the Washington Memorial Library in Macon, where I had spent many happy hours during my childhood devouring its book collection to enlarge my window on the world. The archivist, Chris Stokes, did a thorough search of Macon City Directories.[2] He informed me, much to my surprise, that a handful of Chinese immigrants had indeed lived in Macon long before my parents came in 1928, and all of them had operated laundries.[3] In fact, according to the city directory, Chinese immigrants as far back as 1885 had operated the Sam Lee Laundry at 533 Mulberry Street that our family would later run.

While searching an archive of photographs of places in Georgia, I stumbled upon a 1906 postcard with a photograph of the 500 block of Mulberry Street that featured the Lanier Hotel, the largest hotel in the region at that time.

When I first examined the postcard that showed the Lanier Hotel, I thought it had been mislabeled because the building pictured did not look like the hotel that I knew. It turned out that I did not recognize the hotel because, sometime before the 1940s, its facade had changed -- with the removal of the balconies in front of the hotel shown on the postcard.

More importantly for me was that, immediately to the right of the hotel, I saw a clear image of the very building that housed the laundry my parents acquired in 1928 above which was a two-room storage area that our family used as meager living quarters until the early 1950s. In fact, this building was undoubtedly the site of the Sam Lee Laundry as far back as 1885.

Sam Lee Laundry, 533 Mulberry Street, 1953.

It was exhilarating to find this 1906 postcard, which showed a horse-drawn buggy and a streetcar running down Mulberry Street in front of the Lanier Hotel, a place that held great sentimental value for me because I spent many happy moments examining and buying a few of the many comic books displayed in the hotel lobby newsstand.

Even though I had seen city directory listings that indicated that a Chinese laundry had been at that address as early as 1885, seeing this photograph of Mulberry Street in 1906 with the building holding the Sam Lee Laundry was definitely more compelling evidence than a listing in a directory.

Murder on Mulberry Street

I made a startling discovery of a quite different nature in 2013 about the tragic fate of a Chinese laundryman in Macon in 1885. I was reading *Three Tough Chinamen* by Scott Seligman,[4] an excellent account of the lives of three Moy brothers who settled in parts of the Midwest during the late 19th century and became influential leaders in Chinese communities in several cities. A footnote in the book referred to a murder one night in 1885 of a relative of the Moys who had a laundry in Macon. The case was never solved, but it was suspected that highbinders, hit men from a Chinese tong,[5] had been sent from Chicago to kill the relative.

Intrigued by this story, I searched archival newspapers and found an article that stated the murdered Chinese laundryman on Mulberry Street was named Sam Lee. This was an unsettling finding because there was only one Chinese laundry on Mulberry Street, the Sam Lee Laundry. The inescapable conclusion was that the murder victim had operated the very same laundry that some 40 years later my parents acquired and above which our family lived. Fortunately, I did not know about this tragedy during the years we occupied the building.

A discovery of historic significance

Chris Stokes unearthed and sent me a 1910 Macon newspaper article that reported the exclusion of a 13-year old

Chinese girl, Mei Ling Soong, from attendance at a white middle school in Macon because she was considered an "alien." This was not surprising in view of the racial prejudice of the place and time, but is noteworthy because of who Mei Ling Soong would become in the future.

Fast forward 33 years to 1943, when Mei Ling, the little Chinese girl who was not allowed to attend a white school in Macon, returned as Madame Chiang Kai-shek, one of the most prominent and admired women of her day in the world, to receive an honorary doctorate from Wesleyan College, the world's oldest college for women.

I still have a vivid memory of this historic occasion as my three siblings, and I, only 6 years old, as the only Chinese children in Macon, were paraded out on a hot and humid Georgia summer day to attend this ceremony. In retrospect, I realize it was a significant moment in history for Chinese in America. Perhaps this brush with history in some unknown way planted a curiosity in me about this history, with which I now am so intrigued.

Madame Chiang Arrives at Wesleyan

Little Mayling Soong comes back to Wesleyan as Madame Chiang Kai-shek, First Lady of China.

Madame Chiang Kai-shek' 1943 visit to Macon, and admiring crowd.

A website for *Southern Fried Rice* paid big dividends

By the early 2000s, website companies had developed software that enabled individuals with little or no technical knowledge to create their own websites. I didn't know anything about how to create a website, but enjoyed tackling the task, even if often on a hit-or-miss basis. Fortunately, many people on the Lulu discussion board offered generous assistance wherever questions arose.

I created a free website on *tripod.com* and, even though it was not high-powered by later standards, it gave me an opportunity to post some of my writings about our family's isolated existence in Macon. Most of my posts were drafts of topics that I would later incorporate into what would become the memoir titled, *Southern Fried Rice: Life in A Chinese Laundry in the Deep South.*

My first website for *Southern Fried Rice* on tripod.com.

Website led to two strokes of good fortune

My website was "discovered" by two people interested in the history of Chinese in Georgia. One was the preeminent scholar on the history of Chinese American women, University of California at Santa Cruz Professor Emerita Judy Yung, and the other was someone at the beginning of his career, a doctoral student, Daniel Bronstein, at Georgia State University who was writing a dissertation on the history of Chinese in Atlanta, Augusta, and Savannah.

Both contacted me via email, for different reasons, at about the same time. Yung was going to Georgia to give some lectures on her field of expertise. She had stumbled upon my website and, noting that I grew up in Macon, thought I might be able to recommend some historic sites that were relevant to Chinese American history. To be honest, I could not think of a single site or place of relevance to Chinese Americans for her to visit other than Wesleyan College in Macon where Madame Chiang Kai-shek had received her honorary doctorate in 1943 during her historic visit to the United States to raise financial and political support for China in its fight against the Japanese invaders. However, the building where that ceremony was held had burned to the ground some years earlier!

After some agonizing, I took advantage of her contact with me to mention my memoir to her, and offered to send a copy of a draft. Yung graciously agreed to read it when she could find time. Fortunately, the story held enough interest for her and after she read the draft, she realized it had some promise and proceeded to give me substantial feedback and encouragement.

Bronstein also happened upon my website and was quite excited to find someone who had some firsthand knowledge of the Chinese living in Georgia back in the middle of the 20th century. As luck would have it, his graduate school mentor, Professor Krystyn Moon, was a program chair for the Association for Asian American Studies, which was holding its annual national conference in Atlanta in the spring of 2006 and was eager to include presentations of research about Chinese in the South. After Bronstein told her about my work, she invited me to submit a paper about Chinese in the American South. As I was not a trained historian, I would not ordinarily have felt sufficiently qualified to submit a proposal to this conference. However, I felt I could say something meaningful on the topic of Chinese experiences in the South. I submitted a proposal, which was accepted, about 19 Chinese descendants of my great grandfather who ran laundries in the Deep South starting in the early 1900s.

So, although the reasons why Yung and Bronstein contacted me were quite different, I was able to get them both to read a draft of my memoir, *Southern Fried Rice*. Fortunately, both found that the memoir had merit. I daresay that, without these two important contacts, I might never have gotten very far along in my "post-retirement career" writing about Chinese American history. Their interest and encouragement gave me a powerful motivation and heightened confidence that what I was doing was of value.

Writing a book is not easy, but creating a suitable cover is also challenging. There is truth to the saying, you can't judge a book by its cover, but in reality, many people do. It is crucial that you have an interesting and eye-catching cover so that potential readers will at least notice your book. My first attempt at creating a cover for *Southern Fried Rice,* not surprisingly, was rather amateurish and humdrum at best. Fortunately, I later had the benefit of the artistic talent of my niece's 15-year-old daughter in designing my cover.[6]

Marketing *Southern Fried Rice*

Southern Fried Rice cover.

After I published *Southern Fried Rice*, I searched for venues or locations where I could market the book. Even though the book would be listed on the Internet on Lulu.com as well as on Amazon.com, how would potential readers know about it? Clearly I needed some more direct method of reaching interested readers. I assumed, rightly or wrongly, that the large chain bookstores would not be likely to want to stock a book that might appeal mainly to a small segment of the population, such as Chinese Americans, so I never even approached them.

Instead, I considered organizations with a primary focus on Chinese Americans. First, I contacted the Chinese Historical Society of America (CHSA) in San Francisco in hopes that they would take some copies to sell on consignment in the small book section of their museum in the heart of Chinatown. Much to my surprise, I was invited to do a book reading, followed by book signing, in 2006. This was much better than I had dreamed possible.

Southern Fried Rice talk, Chinese Historical Society of America, San Francisco.

I had actually never attended a book reading in person although I had watched many talks on a literary program on C-SPAN on cable television. I pondered the best way to present my talk. Since I had always learned more from authors who spoke conversationally about their books than those who read extensive passages verbatim, I was inclined to avoid the latter approach. But I felt that potential buyers would want to hear some sections read word for word to give them a feel for my writing style. I compromised and decided I would be more comfortable if I kept the verbatim reading to a minimum and spent more time talking about the background and purpose of the book. My sisters, Mary and Eugenia (Jean), came with me to provide moral support. The event was well attended, with about 50 in the audience, including several friends, and their response was positive, much to my relief. I even sold and signed more than a handful of books!

KTVU-TV interview

Thanks to the press releases from the Society, another surprise was that in 2006 Rosy Chu of KTVU-TV invited me for an interview on her program, *Bay Area People,* a local television talk show. I had never done a television interview so it was exciting to be invited but also a bit scary thinking about it! It would be taped, but still I would have to be well prepared as there would be no re-takes.

After mulling it over, I decided to just "go for it," as it would be a great learning experience (in case I got subsequent invitations). I recognized it would be a good way to promote the book, but then I had real doubts as I later learned that the program aired at 6:30 in the morning. Who watches talk shows at 6:30 in the morning?

On the day of the interview, I flew in from Southern California and arrived a bit early just to be sure I could find the studios of the station in Oakland. As I sat alone in the lobby waiting, a young couple from the Society for the Prevention of Cruelty to Animals entered with two dogs. As I began to realize that they were also going to be on the program, I started to feel defeated. How could I possibly compete with two cute furry guests! A third guest arrived who was a "swap meet" or "flea market" junkie who was going to show off some of her treasures.

Just as the show was about to start, I asked myself, was this experience going to be a disaster (for me)? Had I made a wise decision in coming 400 miles to be on a 30-minute program with three guests? The realization that I would only have about eight minutes of airtime at best galvanized me for the interview. During the few minutes before the session started, I told myself to make the most of my eight minutes on the show and be as articulate, informed, and charming as I could be. Moreover, I deliberately spoke faster than I usually do to squeeze in more comments.

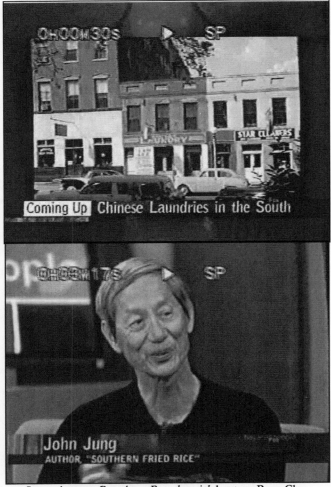

Interview on *Bay Area People with* hostess Rosy Chu.

Fortunately, I got to be the first guest, which lowered my anxiety. Moreover, each guest appeared on the set individually so I did not have to sit next to the SPCA couple with the two cute dogs or with the Queen of Swap Meets. The interview went smoothly, and I survived the test! In fact, after I got to see the tape, I thought I did rather well and to generate some additional publicity I later posted it on YouTube.[2]

One lesson this experience taught me was that you have to take chances. *Carpe diem,* seize the day (or the opportunity), if you want to succeed in whatever you do!

Association for Asian American Studies (AAAS)

The Association for Asian American Studies sent press releases about its 2006 spring conference in Atlanta to local Asian American groups such as the Organization of Chinese Americans (OCA) to invite their participation. Dennis Chao, its president, learned that I would be giving a talk at the conference and contacted me to ask if I would speak at a dinner meeting of the OCA. This seemed like a great opportunity to talk about my memoir, *Southern Fried Rice,* at a place not far from the setting of our family story and where my cousins and their families still lived.

However, right from the start, the dinner event seemed doomed because, as I later learned, a miscommunication had occurred between the OCA and the restaurant. Many more people had signed up for the talk than the restaurant thought, so there was a mad scramble at the last minute to get and cook enough food to serve. By some miracle, they managed to somehow prepare the dinner, but not without a considerable delay.

During dinner, for which I had lost any appetite, I realized that I needed to condense my 50-minute talk to about 15 minutes because by the time I got to speak it would be late into the evening. Somehow this potential fiasco turned into a triumph of sorts. After my condensed 15 minute talk, the Q&A ran on and on until I finally cut it off after 45 minutes. I then realized that my topic held strong interest, at least for Chinese in the South, and I would later learn it had strong appeal elsewhere as well. Having survived this crisis, I gained a confidence that I could handle any future obstacles at presentations, of which I would later experience many at subsequent talks.

Right to left: Cousin Hoi Lam, his wife Sue, my sister Mary, and Kwan family.

Two unexpected dividends of the OCA talk

During the conference, I received two unexpected offers to return to Atlanta to speak at the end of the following month. First, Sachi Koto, a former CNN news anchor who became a successful business consultant with her own company, invited me to be the keynote speaker at a forthcoming event in Atlanta. The event, Who's Who Among Asian Americans in Georgia, would recognize and honor an assemblage of 67 of the "best and brightest" Asian Americans in business, science, and academia at a black tie event at the Omni Hotel in Atlanta.

I was startled to receive this invitation out of the blue. I had only met Koto a few minutes earlier so I was puzzled as to why I would receive this honor. I hesitated, but did not decline, telling her I would need a little time to think about it. A few days later, she contacted me again to see if I had decided. Her follow-up call convinced me that this was a serious offer! I was still not sure what I was getting myself into but I reasoned that if she wanted me to speak, it was her choice; it was not as if I had been applying for the role. Thus, I felt less pressure than if I were seeking the opportunity. Despite some reservations, I decided to accept the offer, recognizing that it was the gift of a golden opportunity to gain exposure for my book and for me.

After my aforementioned talk at the OCA dinner I had another unexpected offer. Following the Q&A, Brenda Tran, president of the local chapter of the National Association of Asian American Professionals (NAAAP), introduced herself and asked if I would come back to Atlanta to speak to this network of young urban professionals. Again, I was surprised by this good fortune but hesitant to accept the invitation, thinking that this youthful group would have minimal interest in hearing about matters from the distant past and that they might find a speaker on career advancement of greater value.

Undaunted, Tran assured me that my knowledge of how Chinese were regarded in the South in the past was of great interest and value for members of her organization. Thus, reassured, I agreed to return to Atlanta in a month, provided I could speak to her group and to Koto's group on the same weekend so I would only need to make one trip from California to Atlanta. We agreed that I could speak to Tran's NAAAP group on Friday night and to the Who's Who gathering at the Omni Hotel on Saturday evening.

Norman Chu, Maiko Natori, Sachi Koto, John Jung, Brenda Tran at OCA talk.

Talk to National Association of Asian American Professionals, Atlanta, 2006.

During the month between receiving these invitations and the actual events, I kept asking myself, how had all this good fortune befallen me, and what was I going to do to deserve the confidence of these two organizers? The Friday night event with NAAAP, during which I talked about what life had been like for my family growing up in our laundry in Macon, went very smoothly. The large audience of young professionals was attentive as well as complimentary. They felt it was worthwhile to learn about what life was like in the South for an earlier generation of Chinese.

The Saturday night black tie event at the Omni Hotel started well. There were more than 300 guests, including many influential state, city, and community leaders at this event that honored 67 Asian Americans in Georgia who had made outstanding achievements in science, business, academia, and the arts.

I was allotted about ten minutes for my keynote speech so I knew I had to be imaginative and creative in generating an engaging talk in the time I had. I figured that I could attract their interest and hold their attention with my presentation, *All I Really Needed To Know, I Learned In A Chinese Laundry.*

Here is what I said:

Distinguished honorees, ladies and gentlemen:

It is a high honor to have the privilege to speak to you on this wonderful occasion. I am impressed with what a vibrant and energetic sense of community there is today among the Atlanta Asian American community. In contrast, when I was growing up in Macon, we had a much smaller community. As a matter of fact, since our family was the *only* Asian, let alone Chinese, family in town, we WERE the Asian COMMUNITY. *When we moved from Macon to San Francisco in the early 1950s, the entire Macon Chinese community was gone!* The local paper noted the occasion with an editorial with the headline, *"Not a Chinese in our town for first time in a century."* When I first saw the headline, I was surprised because it never occurred to me that there had ever been any Chinese in Macon before us.

A few years ago, as I reflected on my family's life in Macon in cultural isolation for over 25 years as the solitary Chinese family in town during an era of staunch segregation, I was inspired, to write a memoir, *Southern Fried Rice*, to document our family's life experiences so that in this small way I could preserve and share a bit of Chinese American history that few people knew about. There isn't time enough tonight to go into any detail about our family story so instead I want to say a few brief things about some valuable lessons learned from growing up in a Chinese laundry.

Let me BEGIN with what might seem to be a digression: I'll bet none of you knew that this past Thursday was:

National Take Your Child To Work With You Day

The premise underlying such a concept is admirable. It's good for kids to learn what their parents do at work, even if they go just one day. I should note, however, that this doesn't always have an accurate result.

As a personal example, when my son was a youngster, I'd occasionally take him with me to campus. He soon reached the (false) conclusion that work was fun because all he ever saw me do was, to use his words:

Drink coffee, chat with students, and scribble illegibly on the blackboard.

Now when I was growing up, I also had the chance to watch my parents work. In fact, I *worked* with my parents in the laundry, and not just for *one* day a year, but EVERY DAY so that I came to sometimes detest having to work in the laundry, BUT now I must admit it did teach me some valuable lessons. What are some of these "lessons" I "learned" from work in our laundry?

The Nature of Work

1. Work is hard. Ben Franklin, as we all know, said "Early to Bed, Early to Rise…Well, he obviously never talked to a Chinese laundryman for, even though my parents went to bed early and got up early… six days a week, 52 weeks a year…It did not exactly make them any healthier, or wealthier…but perhaps wiser.

2. *If it can go wrong, it will.* This saying also applies in the laundry. When the hired help doesn't come in, the work must still be done. When machinery breaks down, the work must still be done… And, as with President Harry Truman, the buck stops here.
My parents still had to get the work done.

3. The customer always thinks he is right, even when he is wrong. Some customers thought we had lost clothes that they later admitted they had never brought in…but had misplaced or left at home.

4. Golden Rule: Treat customers the way you want to be treated… this did not always work, but it was a good starting point.

5. Learn how to "read" or size up customer. That way I could pick easy-to-serve customers to wait on… and let Father deal with the obnoxious ones.

26

6. Dealing with many illiterate customers, white as well as black, quickly taught me the value of being able to read and write and why education is so important.

7. Learn problem-solving skills:
For example: Lost tickets were the bane of our existence...
By the way, just why the expression, *No tick-ee, no wash-ee,* was used to criticize the laundryman is a mystery to me. No Chinese laundryman ever enforced such a policy because we always found the laundry, even without a ticket. But we had to open, and rewrap, many bundles to find the right clothes.
This taught me to develop strategies for finding a customer's clothes efficiently.

8. Develop organizational and memory skills because Time is Money: In a laundry, you have to do more than just wash and iron clothes; after that you must sort and reassemble finished items for each customer, and to do this efficiently you need to be organized and have a good memory.

9. Money Does Not Grow On Trees, (although it sometimes fell out of clothes).Our parents did not indulge us, but they always found the way to provide for essential needs especially if it had to do with our schoolwork.

10. Family cooperation is essential for survival... we all had to pitch in and work together in order to make a living.

These lessons were invaluable in helping me succeed throughout life.

Now I want to conclude by contrasting two conceptions of Laundry Life. The first, I will call the Customer's "Romantic" Philosophy of The Laundry.

There was an OLD commercial in which a white customer asks the Chinese laundryman: How do you get the shirts so white? The Laundryman's proud but sly answer:

ANCIENT CHINESE SECRET!

Imagine background music of "Laundryman, My Laundryman" to the popular 1910 tune of "Chinatown, My Chinatown." "[8]

In other words, *the white* ad writer imbued CHINESE with magic-like power to transform dirty, smelly clothes into clean fragrant clothes. This stereotype shows that mainstream society saw Chinese as experts, but only in this one area.

Versus

A "Realistic" Philosophy of Laundry, one that might represent the viewpoint of the Chinese laundryman:

Children, you should aspire to something higher than doing laundry; control your own future with knowledge and education. Our laundry earnings will provide the financial support for you to get this valuable education.

In conclusion, we must recognize that, successful though we may be, we did NOT do it alone. We stood on the shoulders of our parents and families, a strength of our Asian cultures.

Tonight, in honoring these 67 outstanding members of the Who's Who Among Asian Americans in Georgia, I think I can safely say that we are at the same time honoring their parents and families who supported them in pursuing and achieving their dreams.

An awful ending to a beautiful evening

Then, after the ceremony and dinner, a disaster struck. With so many people (300 or so) milling around after the dinner and awards ceremony, it was difficult for them to find or even see my book table. Moreover, having already spent $100 per plate for dinner, most people probably didn't have any money left for buying books.

So, there I was, stuck at the Omni Hotel that night with many box loads of unsold books, and 3,000 miles from home! It was a moment of great despair! Fortunately, the event organizer, Koto, kindly offered to store my boxes and boxes of unsold books in her garage until I could develop a plan to retrieve them! As it turned out, although I did not know it at the time, destiny would bring me back to Georgia a few months later and provide me with several opportunities to sell my books.

Omni Hotel Gala with some NAAAP-Atlanta members.

After the Atlanta conference, a trip to Augusta, Georgia, gave me an opportunity to make a pilgrimage to visit the site where my father had worked for several years in the early 1920s shortly after he first arrived in the United States. I got to speak about *Southern Fried Rice* at a potluck dinner at the Chinese Consolidated Benevolent Association (CCBA), an organization in which my father's uncle and cousin were pioneering leaders.

Museum of Chinese in the Americas, New York, 2006

Just as my hope in contacting the CHSA was to get them to display and sell my books, I approached the Museum of Chinese in America (MOCA) with the same modest goal. And, just as I was fortunate that the CHSA responded by inviting me to speak, MOCA's William Dao felt I had a story that was of great interest and extended a similar offer.

Book signing, Museum of Chinese in America, New York, 2006.

We were able to schedule a date close to a weekend when I had already planned to be in New York for a family birthday, so the timing was perfect, especially since I had to pay my travel expenses to New York. The audience included my wife's brother Alan and his family from Toronto as well as my grand niece, Amy, and her husband, Frank, from Brooklyn. I was also pleased that noted psychology professor Kay Deaux, a friend from my graduate school days at Northwestern, came to support me.

When I spoke about the book in New York's Chinatown at the MOCA, and later in 2008 at the Chinese American Museum of Chicago in Chicago's Chinatown, I was surprised how much interest there was in learning about Chinese in the South. For these northern audiences, the attraction had to be somewhat different from that for southern Chinese. I think Chinese in the South found affirmation from my memoir in that my story was similar to their lives, but it had not been told publicly. I was like a hero to them.

In contrast, the lives of Chinese in the South were unfamiliar to many audiences in northern or western cities. For some of them, my stories probably intrigued them from an "anthropological" perspective. They were curious to know how Chinese in the South existed without having a vibrant "Chinatown" with many Chinese stores, restaurants, churches, community organizations, and of course, Chinese people.

A visit to Macon

When my family moved from Macon to San Francisco in 1952, the intent of my parents was to make a permanent move. A primary reason for our family move was that we were the solitary Chinese in town, and my parents felt it was high time for us to live with other Chinese, especially as my two sisters were approaching dating and marriageable age.

As I had never lived anywhere else, I did feel a sense of loss when we left Macon, but after we moved to San Francisco, I was so involved adjusting to such a different place that I didn't think much about the city we had left behind. One reason was that I did not have any close friends in Macon because, although I enjoyed many friendships at school, I had virtually no peer companions or friends to hang out with after school because we lived in the business district.

However, over 50 years later I had the chance to take my wife, Phyllis, to see my hometown in 2004 when our vacation included a visit to see friends at Duke University in North Carolina. We then drove to Atlanta to see some of my relatives, but I had not planned to visit Macon since I had not been in touch with anyone there for decades. But since Phyllis was interested in seeing where I grew up, we made an unannounced 75-mile side trip from Atlanta. At the last minute, I was able to locate my best friend from grammar school, Richard Harris, and arrange a lunch get-together with him. He brought along another junior high classmate, Carey Pickard, and his wife, Beverly, who graciously invited us to stay overnight at their home before returning to Atlanta.

In the morning, the Pickards gave us the grand tour of the town, pointing out many historic buildings and giving details about Macon that I never was aware of when I was growing up there. Touring the historic downtown Macon was a sentimental journey for me. After the more than 50 years since I lived there, some structures like the courthouse, post office, and city hall were more or less the same, whereas most of the movie theatres were gone, and many retail stores were empty and boarded up. The suburbanization trend that led people to desert central parts of cities all over the country did not spare Macon.

Georgia Literary Festival, Macon

Imagine my surprise and delight when I was invited to come speak in Macon in the fall of 2006 when it was selected to host the Georgia Literary Festival. This annual event celebrates writers with some connection to a selected city, either because they lived there at some time or wrote about some aspect of it.

Who would have thought that a timid but smart little son of immigrant parents from China who grew up in their laundry would come back to Macon decades later to a receptive audience of people in his hometown who came to hear his story! The opportunity to speak about *Southern Fried Rice* in Macon, where the story took place, was a highlight of my writing and speaking career.

A popular Macon newspaper columnist, Ed Grisamore, got wind of my impending visit and interviewed me by phone. In this touching excerpt from his column in the *Macon Telegraph* he imagines my ties to Macon where I grew up many decades ago.

> When John Jung stretches his memory across the years and the miles, it takes him to a place far away yet still close to every chamber of his heart.
>
> From his office in the psychology department at California State University in Long Beach, where he is now professor emeritus, Macon is a tether to his past. He was born here and lived in Macon until he was 14 years old. It helped shape him in so many ways, a mental scrapbook filled with joy and pain. It poured the footing and provided the backdrop for a memoir he calls *Southern Fried Rice*.
>
> From 1928 to 1952, the Jungs were the only Chinese family living in Macon. "A minority of one," he said. It was not an easy life, but he had nothing to measure it against. As Chinese, we were neither fish nor fowl, he said. We were just different from everyone else, and we learned to live with that. They operated the Sam Lee Hand Chinese Laundry at 519 Mulberry St., near the old Lanier Hotel, where a new parking deck has been built. He lived upstairs above the laundry with his father, mother, two sisters, and brother.

Grisamore concluded his wistful commentary by reporting that our family left Macon in the mid 1950s to live in San Francisco, where we were no longer the only Chinese in town.

During my visit to Macon for the Georgia Literary Festival, I again reconnected with my best friend from grammar school, Richard Harris. I also got to meet Tim Adams who attended junior high school at the same time I did. I did not know Tim then because I was a year older. However, Tim remembered who I was and graciously contacted me to welcome my return to Macon and to invite me to be a guest at his home during my visit. One evening Richard and Tim invited about 20 people from our junior high class to a lovely party in my honor. This charming "Southern hospitality" made the homecoming especially memorable.

Top two rows: Speaking at the Georgia Literary Festival. Bottom left Chris Stokes, library genealogist, and I. Bottom right: with Carey Pickard, a junior high classmate, and Richard Harris, my best friend in grammar school.

Some surprises in publishing *Southern Fried Rice*

After working for months to finalize *Southern Fried Rice*, the big moment finally arrived and I was ready to upload my files to my print-on demand-printer, Lulu.com. I waited anxiously for several days before the proof copy arrived in the mail. When I ripped open the container, I was amazed at how big the book appeared. But when I inspected the book, I realized, to my embarrassment, that every page was double-spaced, which looks fine for a typed manuscript, but awful in a printed book. So, I had to change the line spacing, re-upload the file, and wait for another proof copy. The consolation was that, with half as many pages, the cost of each book was also substantially reduced!

To be honest, there were other mistakes and problems along the way in formatting the book, such as getting the photographs in the right place, tweaking them so they were suitable for a printed page rather than for a monitor screen, and making sure that they were of high, rather than low, resolution quality. Murphy's Law, "If anything can go wrong, it will," is definitely valid when it comes to writing, editing, and publishing a book!

Imagine my surprise one day to receive an email that at first seemed accusatory! A Chinese American with a name, James Jung, that was eerily similar to mine, wrote to tell me that a friend has told him he should read *Southern Fried Rice*. This chemistry professor went on to tell me that his family's life in a small town in North Carolina during the 1940s was virtually the same as the one I described for our family in Macon during the same time period.

His parents, immigrants from China like mine, ran a laundry. Moreover, like our family, they were the only Chinese family in town. He noted that he, his sister, and his four brothers shared many similar experiences that our family did living in cultural isolation in the South during the days when Jim Crow laws prevailed. He even noted that there was a resemblance between our living space above the laundry and where they lived, even to the detail of each having three front windows above the laundry.

I then realized that my laundry story was not so unique but probably could represent the situation for dozens, if not hundreds, of other Chinese laundry families throughout the U. S. and Canada. In the years since I wrote the book, I have discovered many other Chinese laundry stories from all parts of the country that were very similar to ours.

While he was reading *Southern Fried Rice*, Charles Brittain, an architect in Macon, suddenly realized as he read my description of my cousin in Atlanta, William Lau, that they had been friends and high school classmates in Atlanta. In 2012, I made another small world discovery involving Brittain. I was back in Macon for another literary event that I will discuss later and was staying at the home of my childhood friend, Richard Harris. In one conversation, I mentioned how a Macon architect, Charles Brittain, while reading my memoir recognized my cousin William who had been one of his high school classmates in Atlanta. At that point, Harris revealed that he knew Brittain, as he was the architect who designed the home where I was his guest! Other readers of my memoir have thoughtfully contacted me to speak fondly about their memories of our family. [9]

Cultural isolation is not limited to Chinese

Cultural or ethnic isolation is a common experience that enabled many non-Chinese to identify with my experiences growing up in Georgia. People across a wide range of ethnic and regional backgrounds who read the book felt they had had similar experiences of isolation, which created a connection with me and led them to share their reactions with me.

One woman came up after a talk I gave to tell me that she grew up in Maine, where hers was the sole black family in her hometown. I heard similar expressions from an East Indian woman who grew up and lived in Africa, a Polish woman who grew up in the Midwest, and a Norwegian man who grew up in Minnesota among German and Nordic groups.

I even discovered an archive of letters written to his elementary school teacher by a young Chinese boy in North Dakota in a town where his family was the only Chinese during the 1920s and had a laundry business. By an amazing coincidence, the boy was also named John Jung. His teacher saved all of his letters, which now reside in an archive called, *John Jung Letters*, [10] at the University of North Dakota! I compared these letters that he *sent* to his teacher with those that I *received* from Macon friends after I moved away. I discussed the common experiences of these two John Jungs in dealing with being the only Chinese in their communities, in a free downloadable document. [11]

In retrospect

Fate smiled on me soon after I published *Southern Fried Rice*. Within months, I had unexpected opportunities for book talks and signings at varied venues in San Francisco, Atlanta, Augusta, Macon, and New York. These experiences were invaluable. First, they reassured me that I could deliver talks to diverse audiences effectively, and that I could handle all types of unexpected mishaps connected with presentations to live audiences -- ranging from equipment malfunctions to poor publicity.

Secondly, it is one thing to write a book, but quite a different matter to sell it. Brick-and-mortar bookstores are reluctant to stock books from unknown authors. Besides, they demand a large discount around 55 percent. At that level, I calculated that I would lose money on every book I sold. Online sales provide a profit, but unless people know about your books, they may not discover them on the Web.

I realized from my experience at book talks that they would be a more effective method to market my books. If I engaged my audience with my talk, many would want to buy an autographed copy for themselves or as gifts.

Endnotes

[1] Walter Bragg. "Not A Chinese in Our Town For First Time in A Century." *Macon News,* March 6, 1956, 4.

[2] I met Chris Stokes several years later when I had the opportunity to speak at the Georgia Literary Festival in Macon. He surprised me with his discovery from a 1952 school yearbook that his father and I had been junior high classmates even though we did not know each other!

[3] Using newspaper archives, I wrote a document about these early Chinese laundrymen in Macon. http://chineselaundry.wordpress.com/2014/06/16/chinese-laundries-of-macon-georgia-1885-1956/

[4] Scott D. Seligman. "Three Tough Chinamen." Hong Kong: Earnshaw Books, Ltd., 2012.

[5] Tongs were Chinese organizations that had several functions for Chinese immigrants, helping govern communities and assisting new immigrants, but they also acted as mafia-like groups that resorted to violence to control gambling, prostitution, and opium dens.

[6] Lauren Doege, the artistic 15-year old daughter of my niece, Liz Gee, offered to design my cover. One of my college students gushed, it's so edgy! I assumed that "edgy" was high praise, and proceeded to use it, and have never regretted it!

7 https://www.youtube.com/watch?v=I-FR8UdYdRk

8 http://en.wikipedia.org/wiki/Chinatown,_My_Chinatown

9 Another reader suddenly realized she knew my sister Mary when she read my mention of my sister Mary's marriage. The reader's mother and my sister Mary had worked together for many years to develop Chinese language classes where they lived. They had lost track of each other after each moved to different places. After reading the memoir, Julius S. in Portland, Oregon, wrote that his father had been one of our customers in Macon. Naomi, a classmate of my sister Mary came to my talk in Macon. My visit enabled them to get reconnected via email after several decades.

10 *John Jung Letters,* University of North Dakota Special Collection: OGL#995 http://webapp.und.edu/dept/library/Collections/og995.html

11 John Jung. "Isolated Chinese Boys And Their White Mentors: Letters From John Jung (1929-1936) and To John Jung (1952-1956)." Association of Asian American Studies Conference. Chicago, IL. April 18, 2008. http://tinyurl.com/q6gmrha

3 Chinese Laundries

Southern Fried Rice, being a memoir, could have been written without extensive details and documentations about the history of Chinese in America. Nonetheless, as writing my memoir progressed, my curiosity and scholar's habits from years as a professor compelled me to do extensive research about this history. I was surprised to discover the large extent to which Chinese operated laundries in the late 1800s and much of the 1900s before this livelihood became increasingly obsolete with the wider availability of affordable home washing machines after World War II. As a kid, growing up in our laundry in Georgia, how was I to know that all across the U. S. (and Canada) there was least one Chinese laundry in virtually every town?

More importantly, I came to realize some of the reasons that the laundry was so commonplace among Chinese immigrants. It was not because it was their preference, or that they had expertise as laundrymen acquired before they left China. Underlying their relegation to this occupational niche was the racism toward Chinese, which drove them out of other work opportunities, and eventually challenged their existence even in the laundry business.

A prequel to *Southern Fried Rice*?

This realization of how pervasive Chinese laundries were, the unavailability of other work for Chinese for many years, and the vital role they had in providing economic survival of the early Chinese led me to publish *Chinese Laundries: Tickets to Survival on Gold Mountai*n in 2007. Writing this book gave me a deeper understanding of why my father, his uncle, his brother, his cousin, and thousands of other Chinese men entered the laundry business even though none of them ever did their own laundry back in their villages in China. As elsewhere, laundry work was considered a domestic responsibility of women in the family.

Chinese Laundries: Tickets to Survival on Gold Mountain.

A total of 19 descendants of my great grandfather, Fun Fai Lo, as shown in the chart below, operated laundries in Georgia, Tennessee, and Alabama. Three of his grandsons left China to seek a living on Gold Mountain at the beginning of the twentieth century. Gan Heung Lo went to Chattanooga, Tennessee, Gan Lion Lo went to Birmingham, Alabama, and Gan Hong Lo went to Augusta, Georgia. What is not known is whether they worked in other parts of the country before they went to the South or whether other relatives helped them get settled.

My father, Kwok Fui Lo, one of 14 great grandsons of Fun Fai Lo, eventually settled in Macon, Georgia after first working in a laundry in Chattanooga for a year or two with the help of his grand uncle, Gan Heung Lo and then in Augusta with the aid of another grand uncle, Gan Hong Lo. He then helped bring his brother, Jew Shiu Dunn, to Macon for a year in 1936 to teach him how to run a laundry business. Then my uncle moved to Atlanta where he opened his own laundry.

This process of chain migration in which Chinese immigrants who had already come to the U. S. helped other family members come to help with the family business was typical for Chinese immigrants all across the country. They might also loan or pool money to enable a newcomer to buy his own laundry.

Competition between Chinese and whites for work led to the passage of the Chinese Exclusion Act in 1882, which denied entry to Chinese laborers but allowed merchants and their families to come. Some Chinese merchants returning from visits to China would claim nonexistent sons, creating "slots" that they could later sell to Chinese laborers seeking to come to the United States. This procedure of purchasing false identity papers often led to blood relatives having different surnames. These immigrants came to be known as "paper sons."

The 19 Chinese Laundries of Fun Fai Lo in the South

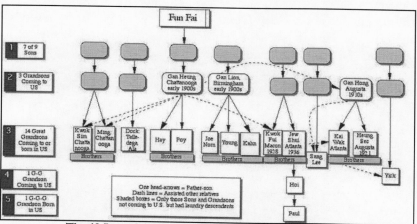

The 19 Laundries of Fun Fai Lo, my great grandfather.

It was sadly true that many Chinese immigrants, whether they worked in a laundry or some other occupation, lived "bachelor lives," either being unmarried and with few prospects for marriage, or were separated from their wives, and in many cases, children left behind in China.

There were, however, some Chinese who managed to come over with wives and children. Others return briefly to get married, while others found a wife, Chinese or of another race, in the United States. An important question is "What was life like for the children who grew up in and helped with the daily work of their parents' laundries?" I had already written about my own experiences in *Southern Fried Rice*, but I wanted to see how similar or different were the experiences of a sample of other "children of Chinese laundries." I searched for, and managed to recruit Chinese from diverse regions of the country, and two from Canada, to write about their experiences and their family life.

My *Chinese Laundries* book combines an analysis of the conditions that led so many Chinese in the late 19th and early 20th centuries to engage in the laundry business, with personal retrospective accounts of laundry life written by several persons who, like me, had grown up in laundries.

I did not want to assume that every Chinese from a laundry life would have the same experiences and feelings, so it was important to obtain accounts from several other Chinese with a laundry background. I also wanted to choose people from laundries located in different parts of the country so that the observations would not be limited to one region.

Fortunately, I had several contacts made at past events. The first person I recruited was Liz Chan, who I had met in San Francisco a few years earlier. She was, perhaps, the first person to buy *Southern Fried Rice*, which had just been published. I remembered her because when I was autographing her copy, she mentioned that she was especially interested in my book because her family had owned a laundry in Louisville, Kentucky.

Another prospect I invited to write was Donna Wong, an administrator at Emory University who I met when I spoke in Atlanta in 2006. I recalled her mentioning that she grew up in a laundry located in Los Angeles.

When I informed my long-time friend, fellow psychology professor Rod Wong, in Vancouver, that I was looking for people who grew up in a laundry to share their experiences in my book, he put me in touch with Elwin Xie, whose family owned a laundry on Pender Street near Vancouver's Chinatown.

Another person I recruited, Lucy Wong Leonard, heard about my talk at the San Diego Chinese Historical Museum and, although she was unable to attend, she contacted me several times by email. From these exchanges she learned I was looking for laundry stories and she wanted to contribute her memories from her family experiences in their Los Angeles laundry.

I found other contributors using suggestions from various contacts, such as Laura Meyers-Chin who came from a Brooklyn laundry background, William Eng who grew up in a New Jersey laundry, and Ken Lee, a professor at Ohio State University, who came from a New York laundry background.

In my appeal for potential contributors, I noted, "What you can contribute is a description of your perceptions, feelings, and experiences as a child from a Chinese laundry background." Although all contributors wrote independently, there was a remarkably high level of agreement about many aspects of the experiences of laundry families regardless of what part of the country the laundry was in. The consensus was that the hours were long and the work was exhausting. Children made their contributions to the operation in different roles, depending on their age, but invariably they had to serve also as go-betweens who translated or mediated between customers and parents who had limited English language skills.

Why were there so many Chinese laundries?

NO LAUNDRIES IN CHINA.

"It's the funniest thing to me," said an old sea captain who for many years was in the China trade, as he settled himself comfortably in his chair and blew a few rings of smoke into the air, "that nine out of every ten Chinamen who come to this country open laundries and engage in a business which does not exist in their native land.

As everyone knows, the Chinese at home wear soft cotton and woolen garments, according to the season, and there is not a pound of starch in all China. Stiffly starched clothes are unknown, and the Chinese men do not do the washing, as they do in this country. Neither is there any regular laundry in the Flowery Kingdom. Therefore it is more than passing strange that Chinamen should all come to America to engage in a trade so foreign to their home industries."

No laundries in China comment in a white laundry trade journal.

Example of the hostility toward Chinese in America leading to their exclusion.

I am sometimes asked at talks why so many Chinese immigrants "chose" to enter the laundry business. In reality, they had little choice, as they were excluded from virtually every type of work available by white labor organizations intent on restricting the Chinese in their economic opportunities. By the late 1800s, laundries were the most common form of self-employment among Chinese, and would remain so for a few decades.

Later, more white-owned steam laundries opened that provided stiff competition for Chinese hand laundries. Furthermore, laws were passed and license fees imposed that favored white laundries. One such law in 1880 prohibited laundries in wooden buildings in San Francisco without a permit. The law made sense in that wood buildings were more susceptible to fires, but since all Chinese laundries occupied wooden structures, the Chinese challenged the fairness of the law when one laundryman, Yick Wo, was jailed for refusing to pay a fine because he did not have a permit. The U. S. Supreme Court ruled in Yick Wo's favor, viewing it as an infringement of the Equal Protection Clause of the 14th Amendment to the Constitution, in Yick Wo v. Hopkins 1885.[1]

Chinese laundrymen worked long hours, and lived in their laundries to make ends meet. White laundry owners protested against these practices, leading to laws against working all night or living in the laundry, to counter the Chinese dominance in the laundry business.

Chinese laundrymen were not entirely free from fault, as the presence of laundries meant disposal of dirty wash water in the streets, creating public hazards to health and safety.

White laundry ad against Chinese laundries, Dothan AL., 1915.

They were often victims of racism in various forms. White youths engaged in pranks and harassment of laundrymen, such as throwing rocks to break store windows. Children would throw mud onto washed clothing that was hanging on outdoor clotheslines.

More serious harm directed at Chinese laundrymen occurred from countless robberies, physical assaults, and even homicides. Many such incidents that Chinese suffered were cited in a detailed argument, "A Statement for Non-Exclusion" in 1905 by Patrick J. Healey and Ng Chew Poon, an early Chinese civil rights activist.[2]

Competition increased between white-owned steam laundries and Chinese hand laundries. In addition to promoting laws that disadvantaged Chinese laundries, such as higher license fees, white laundries also resorted to scare tactics in advertisements that questioned the hygienic conditions in Chinese laundries where the laundrymen ate and slept in the laundry.

Not only were their workloads heavy, but also they had little time to socialize, assuming there were other Chinese in their community. In cities with large Chinese populations, such as Chicago, New York, or San Francisco, the laundrymen had to spread their locations over the city to ensure that they did not compete with each other. This requirement added to their isolation from countrymen, and on Sundays when they did not open their laundries, they would flock to Chinatown where they could congregate, have a Chinese meal, buy Chinese food, and for some, gamble, smoke opium, or visit brothels.

Laundrymen outside cities even more isolated

Chinese who lived in towns where they were the only Chinese or one of a handful of Chinese, had no opportunity to visit Chinatowns, which were too distant to travel to and return home within a single day.

The situation for the 64 Chinese listed in the 1910 census for the state of Iowa, all laundrymen, illustrates the problem in many areas of the country. No county in Iowa had more than four or five Chinese, all men, residing there. The map below shows how well dispersed, or isolated, the Chinese laundrymen in Iowa were.

One way Chinese laundrymen dealt with their isolation was to travel anywhere from a few miles to around 100 miles on a Sunday, their one day when they closed their laundries, to congregate at a centrally located laundry for companionship. In Georgia, laundrymen in small towns close to Atlanta would occasionally convene there on Sundays for companionship. My father would take me with him on the train to Atlanta, a two-hour trip each way, for this purpose. The virtual absence of Chinese women in the first waves of immigrants ensured that most of the men were bachelors or if married, had come without their wives and children, who were left behind in China.

Distribution of Chinese laundrymen across Iowa, 1910.

A photograph I found on the Internet showed about six to eight middle-aged and older Chinese men in a large room. In this candid photograph, some were seated while others were standing, but all appeared to be eating. It may well have been a work break as some of the men were attired in their undershirts. I imagined this type of scene with only men in the photograph was commonplace during the years of the bachelor society imposed by the Chinese Exclusion Act.

I posted the photograph on a Facebook group page with mostly Chinese American members, asking if anyone could guess what the photograph represented. My assumption was that many contemporary viewers would not appreciate the meaning of the photograph of an all-male gathering. Within a matter of minutes, Raymond Douglas Chong posted a similar photograph from the 1930s on Facebook that showed eleven Chinese men seated around a makeshift table. These laundrymen were gathered for a meal and companionship at the Sun Tong Laundry in Santa Barbara. Several men were wearing neckties, so it is likely they dressed up to travel from outlying areas on a Sunday when their laundry would be closed.

Chinese laundrymen socialize at a meal, Sun Tong Laundry, Santa Barbara, California, in the 1930s. Courtesy, Raymond Douglas Chong.

It was highly improbable, but a few minutes later, Kelvin Han Yee, an actor in Los Angeles, posted a cropped version of the identical photograph to the Facebook group. Chong and Yee, each had family ties to the Chinese who ran this laundry, and both responded almost immediately to my Facebook post.[3]

Chinese Laundries book talk experiences

One thing I learned about the audiences at my talks about the Chinese laundries book was that about a third to a half of them had parents or other relatives who ran laundries. A few even grew up and helped with the work in their parents' laundries. During Q&A, occasionally they would share their own laundry experiences or confirm some of the observations I had made. I was gratified that they came to my talk and I found it rewarding that they were interested. At first I was a bit puzzled about their interest insofar as I was not telling them anything that they did not already know from their own experiences or stories from their parents. Then it finally dawned on me that they were pleased that someone knowledgeable about their experiences was telling their story of what the laundry life was like. Often, some people would ask me to sign a copy of the book with an inscription to their children.

On several occasions someone would ask whether a specific laundry in say, Nebraska or Texas, for example, was cited in the book and I had to disappoint them by noting that there were hundreds, if not thousands, of Chinese laundries! However, on one occasion when the question was raised as to whether the book included a relative's laundry in San Mateo, California, I responded by asking for the name of the laundry because I remembered I did include one from that city. When she gave me the name, I realized that for once I could say, yes. I took a copy of the book, and after a few moments, turned to a page that contained a photograph of that very laundry, and showing it to her, asked, "Is this your laundry?" Needless to say, she was quite surprised!

Designing the Chinese Laundries book cover

I felt it would be fitting to include two iconic images - an abacus and a laundry ticket - on the cover of *Chinese Laundries: Tickets to Survival on Gold Mountain*.[4] As luck would have it, the laundry ticket I used from my uncle's Atlanta laundry also included Chinese characters next to the English words for each type of clothing.

I was surprised to receive an email from someone who could read Chinese and had examined the laundry list on the book cover closely. He had studied the Chinese characters on the ticket next to "overalls" and wondered if his translation of those characters as "greasy clothes" was correct. However, since I cannot read (or write) Chinese I was not sure, even though my intuition told me he was probably correct. I knew that in Chinese, where there is no existing equivalent for an English word, a term is often coined. For example, *dai fow* or big city stands for San Francisco, since it had the largest Chinese population. I did check with someone who does read Chinese and he confirmed the conclusion of the careful scrutinizer of my book cover!

Connecting with *Chinese Laundries* readers via the Web

Many Chinese immigrants to other countries in the last part of the 19th century were from the same areas in Toishan where many Chinese in North America came from. Moreover, many of them found similar work, in railroad construction, mining, laundries, farming, grocery stores, and restaurants. The power of the Internet has enabled me to communicate with people interested in Chinese laundries even across the Pacific with Chinese in Hong Kong, Taiwan, New Zealand, and Australia.

Thus, I learned much about the similarities of the lives of Chinese in New Zealand and North America through my contact on the Internet with Helen Wong, an active researcher in New Zealand on the Chinese diaspora. She created links to my books on a wiki site about Overseas Chinese.[5]

Another example of the potential for connections via the Internet is this 2013 email from a writer-journalist in New Delhi, Marina Bang. I believe I was as thrilled to receive it as she was to have discovered my book, *Chinese Laundries.*

"I was thrilled to come across your website during a search for "Chinese laundries," and read many of your entries with great interest. I have now ordered your books Chinese Laundries and Sweet and Sour and am looking forward to their arrival. I am a South African but lived in

Hong Kong for almost a decade where I worked as a journalist on the South China Morning Post."

Why have Chinese laundries disappeared into history?

At the end of the 19th century, the Chinese laundry business was peaking. Chinese found a new economic avenue, restaurants, as the nation increasingly became an urban rather than a rural society. More people in cities began to eat some of their meals at restaurants. Moreover, an Americanized version of Chinese food became attractive to non-Chinese as an inexpensive as well as somewhat exotic dining experience.

Laundrymen encouraged their children to get an education that would enable them to find more lucrative and less physically demanding white collar or professional careers. When the parents retired, their children did not want or need to continue the family laundry. With their higher education, and wider acceptance of Chinese in fields previously barred to them, they pursued higher paying work in professional fields.

Additional factors that drove the nails into the coffin, so to speak, for Chinese laundries was the affordability of washers and dryers designed for the home soon after the 1950s, and the development of permanent-press clothes and polyester fabrics in the 1960s that required little or no ironing.

Endnotes

[1] http://supreme.justia.com/cases/federal/us/118/356/case.html

[2] https://archive.org/details/statementnonexclu00heal

[3] http://chineselaundry.wordpress.com/2014/03/05/connections-with-the-past-with-a-modern-tool-facebook/

[4] I again enlisted the talents of my grandniece, Lauren Doege, who created the Southern Fried Rice cover, to design one for this book.

[5] http://chinese.rootswiki.legacy1.net/doku.php?id=history:united_states

4 Chopsticks in the Land of Cotton

Old times there are not forgotten.......

Given that I had never been in Mississippi, how did I come to write a book in 2008 about Chinese grocery store families in the Mississippi Delta? Well, technically speaking, I had been in Mississippi back in the early 1950s when I took a train from New Orleans late one summer evening en route to Macon, Georgia. When I awoke the next morning, the train was in Alabama, so obviously I must have previously been in Mississippi, physically speaking, although asleep.

First, a digression is needed to explain how a talk I presented in Los Angeles about *Southern Fried Rice* ended up with me writing a book about Mississippi Delta Chinese, *Chopsticks in the Land of Cotton*. At the time, I was seeking venues where I could speak about *Southern Fried Rice* to promote the book. Living near Los Angeles, in 2007 I decided to approach the Chinese Historical Society of Southern California, although I was not sure if they would be interested in inviting me to speak since my topic would be Chinese life in the American South. But judging from a list of their past speakers, they did not limit their speakers to authors writing about Chinese in Southern California. I contacted them, and I was pleasantly surprised when they invited me to speak in Chinatown in Los Angeles. [1]

What do you know about the Chinese in Mississippi?

During the Q&A after the talk, an audience member, Roland Chow, stood up and identified himself as a Chinese from Mississippi. He had learned of the talk at the last minute and came because he was eager to learn about my life in Georgia. He wanted to know if I was familiar with the history of Chinese in the Mississippi Delta. I acknowledged that I had read two books about them but had never had direct contact with these Chinese aside from meeting one student from the Delta when we were both attending the University of California at Berkeley.

He felt that my experiences growing up in Georgia closely resembled his own in Greenville, Mississippi, and he urged me to consider writing a book about the history of the Mississippi Delta Chinese. I was taken aback by this suggestion, which came out of the blue. And, certainly, deciding to write a book about people in a place that I hardly knew much about is not something I would immediately jump into. I politely thanked Chow and said it was a project that I would have to give some thought to before I could make any commitment.

Chow was determined to persuade me, and offered me the names and phone numbers of several Chinese in or from the Delta who would be happy to talk with me. A month or two later, I did follow up on his leads and found the idea of writing a book on this unique population was worthwhile. There were two excellent previous books written about the Delta Chinese, one that was a scholarly sociological analysis and one that was an ethnography using many interviews with different segments of the Delta Chinese community.[2] However, they had been published about 30 years earlier, so it seemed time to take a newer look.

With Roland Chow, who urged me to write about the Delta Chinese.

If it had not been for Chow's suggestion, however, I very much doubt I would have decided to work on this topic on my own initiative. It was simply a lucky thing that he found out about my talk and came that evening!

I realized that the history of these Chinese was unique and important to document. The Chinese grocery stores were fast vanishing with the changing times. The older generation was getting smaller due to retirements and deaths. The younger generation, with the benefit of college educations, had little interest in continuing with these family businesses as they had prospects for better employment opportunities.

In researching background material for writing a social history of Mississippi Delta Chinese grocers, I conducted phone interviews and incorporated several types of material ranging from academic scholarly work to several other published accounts about the Delta Chinese grocers.

I made use of the Library of Congress American Memory photograph collection created during the Great Depression by acclaimed photographers for the federal agency, Works Projects Administration (WPA) to document the lives of everyday people in the Delta as well as the stores and residential buildings in the community. I used several excellent images from this resource that added to the readers' visualization of the stores, towns, farms, and people in the community.

There is an interesting story associated with one of these photographs that I used of a dilapidated looking grocery store from sometime in the 1930s located in Altheimer, Arkansas. I had recently been in contact by email with a Chinese American with a grocery store background in Altheimer, Arthur Hsu. On a whim, I sent the photograph to him just to see if he remembered the store, not thinking that it might be a Chinese-owned store because it was named the Benson store. To my great surprise, he wrote back declaring that the Benson store was in fact his father's store. When he acquired this business from someone named Benson, he just never bothered to change the signage! Hsu was amazed to see the photograph, and wondered how I found it. He recalled sitting on that wood bench in front of the store to cool off on summer evenings with family members, despite the presence of mosquitoes.

Chinese grocery store in Altheimer, Arkansas, 1930s.

The most informative material was a set of about 20 oral histories of Chinese from grocery store families from the Archives at Delta State University in Cleveland, Mississippi, recorded in 1999.[3] Most of the interviewees were about 50 years old. These transcripts provided rich details of the daily lives of Chinese family life not only in store operations but also about the social interactions, relations, and community ties among this small population of less than 1,000 Chinese living miles apart from one another in numerous small Delta towns around the middle of the 20th century.

Reading these transcripts gave me a vivid picture and deeper understanding of what their daily lives were like. I wanted to include direct quotes from some of these documents in my book to illustrate important issues. To make sure that I had not misinterpreted them or taken them out of context, I contacted the respondents so they could examine any materials that I attributed to them. This exchange generated strong interest among Delta Chinese and enthusiasm for a historical account of the Chinese groceries and the families that ran them.

I was struck by the strong feeling of attachment to the Delta that was widespread among the interviewees. I had initially assumed there might be some negative sentiments expressed about living in the segregated South. Of course, people willing to be interviewed are not a cross section of the Chinese, and others who have negative feelings might be reluctant to express them or also may have moved out of the region. In fact, Sam Sue, who grew up near Clarksdale but now lives in New York, wrote a stinging critique of what life was like for Chinese in the Delta when he was a young man.[4] However, I was somewhat surprised that such feelings were rare. Delta Chinese, despite their "between black and white" status, generally held positive views of their lives.

There was some concern among a few respondents that these unedited transcripts contained some mistakes and that the conversational nature of the comments might make the respondents come across as poorly educated and inarticulate. Some even asked if they could revise or edit the transcripts of these interviews from well over 20 years back. I tried to reassure them that no one expects conversations to contain polished statements, free of grammatical flaws, repetitions, and hesitations. And, I insisted that it would not be suitable for my research if they were to now re-write or edit what they had previously said over 20 years ago.

Invitation to speak in the Mississippi Delta, 2008

As word got around to the Chinese in the Mississippi Delta that I was writing a book about their history, some of the long-time residents of the Delta naturally wondered who I was, prompting some to read my memoir about my growing up in Georgia. After reading *Southern Fried Rice*, several influential advocates felt that my southern life experiences resembled many of their own. This feeling that made them comfortable with me, an outsider, writing about them.

As I was already in the final stages of writing, it seemed a bit late to go to the Delta, but at the same time it was, of course, an important opportunity to talk in-person and on-site with people who I was writing about.

Frieda Quon was one of the individuals who was most engaged in this negotiation. She was a librarian at Delta State

University, on the verge of retirement. She grew up in her family's grocery store in Greenville, Mississippi. She had read *Southern Fried Rice* and had a very strong conviction that I could relate to and understand the lives of Delta Chinese, even though I had grown up in Georgia, where we ran a laundry rather than a grocery store. Quon spearheaded a plan to invite me to come to the Delta to give two talks based on *Southern Fried Rice, one* at Delta State University, and another one at a Chinese American Citizens Alliance (C.A.C.A.) dinner in Greenville.

Chinese community leaders wanted me to tour the Delta so I could meet some Delta Chinese in person and get to know about their grocery store lives better than I could from reading documents and books. They were pleased that a book about the Mississippi Delta Chinese grocers was in the works, but they were concerned that phone interviews and oral histories might not give accurate or enough information. I spent 16 days staying with several Chinese hosts across the Delta, supported by other members of the Mississippi C.A.C.A. chapter.

Dilemmas of a tour of the Delta

I was torn about accepting this unexpected invitation. Clearly, on one hand, it would be invaluable to visit the Delta in person even though I was at a stage in my thinking and writing about the Delta Chinese where I felt I had a firm understanding. A visit, however, might show me that my views were not correct and I'd have to rewrite my book. That was a risk that I'd have to take, and was willing to do, but there was a greater risk that I feared. Suppose I went down to the Delta, and while receiving more than a couple of weeks of Southern hospitality as a house guest in towns up and down the Delta, I only got to see and hear the "good side" of the Delta Chinese experience. Would my trip bias me toward seeing only the good images that the hosts might display? And, then if I wrote anything the least bit unflattering about the Delta Chinese, might they feel that I had betrayed them? Nonetheless I realized that the visit would be an invaluable opportunity for me to see the region and meet some of the people that I was writing about. I overcame my anxiety and looked at the trip as a challenge, so I accepted the invitation.

Fortunately, the observations and conversations I had among the Delta Chinese generally were consistent with what I had formulated from my prior research and had already been writing in the book. I did have a few disagreements in discussions on the sensitive topic of racial attitudes, behaviors, and beliefs between Chinese and the whites and blacks. I think I was able to persuade those with objections that any historical analysis of Delta society that ignored racial issues would seem seriously flawed even if the main goal was to depict Chinese family life.

I was seeing only the remnants of the Chinese grocery stores, which were no longer as prevalent as they had been a generation ago. I came away, however, with a better understanding and appreciation of the lives of this unique Chinese community that managed to survive in sometimes harsh circumstances for so long, but was now in decline with the passing of the older generation and the moving of many members of later generations to larger cities such as Memphis, Houston, San Francisco, and Los Angeles.

My C.A.C.A dinner talk in Greenville, Mississippi, 2008.

At the end of this trip, I found time to arrange through a long-time associate, Professor Pamela Banks, to give a presentation about the Mississippi Delta Chinese at Jackson State University, a historically black institution. Banks and I had directed mentoring programs at our respective universities for more than 20 years with funding by the National Institute of Mental Health to recruit minority students interested in pursuing research careers in psychology and related disciplines.

Connection with Paul and Helen Wong

After I had written most of the first draft of my book about the Chinese grocers in the Mississippi Delta, I chanced to learn at a dinner after my Cupertino, California, talk on *Southern Fried Rice* that a Paul Wong, who had lived in the Delta, was also working on a book on this topic. This was a "stop signal" to me because I felt that if a native of the Delta were writing a book on the Delta Chinese, it would have an insider's perspective than I did not have.

I contacted Wong and he clarified that he was editing a collection of reminiscences of Chinese who attended the Chinese Mission School in Cleveland, Mississippi, and was not writing a history of the Chinese grocers and their families in the Delta. We were not working on the same topic, although what he was doing had some connection to the larger story I was working on. With the assurance that we were not trying to write the same book, I continued to research and write *Chopsticks in the Land of Cotton*.

This contact turned out to be fortuitous for other reasons. Helen, Paul's wife, also from the Delta, had just completed writing her own memoir of her family, and a gathering was planned within a few days at their home at which copies of her memoir would be distributed to family members in the area. The Wongs lived only about 25 miles from me in Southern California and they graciously invited me to the event at their home. I was presented with a copy of Helen's family memoir, which told an amazing story.

Joe Young, her father, obtained a civil engineering degree in 1924 from the Massachusetts Institute of Technology, MIT, one of the most prestigious engineering universities in the country. He then went to China to help build railroads, but returned to the U. S. with his family when the dangers of war between China and Japan increased in the late 1930s. He settled in the Delta, certainly the only graduate of MIT to open a grocery store in Tchula, and later in Greenville.

By "accident," I discovered that Helen's grandfather, Joe Guay, and his two brothers had owned a laundry in Holyoke, Massachusetts before 1920. When they heard about opportunities to earn a better living in the Delta running a grocery store, they sold their laundry and moved to the Delta where they operated one of the larger and best known stores, Joe Gow Nue Grocery, at the foot of the main street of Greenville just across from the Mississippi River. I say "by accident" because I was sitting with Wong in his living room, telling him how surprised I was to discover there were no Chinese in the Delta operating laundries whereas it was the primary Chinese business in all other parts of the U. S. at that time. No one I interviewed from the Delta could recall ever seeing a Chinese laundry in the region; yet I knew from census records that, prior to 1910, there had been a handful of Chinese laundries in the Delta.

I suggested to Wong that perhaps some of these earlier Chinese laundrymen saved enough capital to acquire an inventory of goods to open a grocery store. Just at that moment, his wife walked into the room and overheard our discussion. She confirmed my reasoning, using the example of her grandfather and his two brothers who had first owned a laundry, but in Massachusetts, before coming to the Delta to enter the grocery business.

On several later occasions, I relied on Wong as a rich source of invaluable information about the Delta Chinese grocers that gave me a better understanding of the conditions under which they lived and worked. Furthermore, Wong's detailed account of how his family moved around the U. S., from Portland, Oregon, to Fargo, North Dakota, and then to the Delta, gave me more insight about the process by which many other Chinese came from many other parts of the country to settle in the Delta.

Connection with Bobby Joe Moon

I discovered a brief, but moving commentary on a website, US DEEP SOUTH by Bobby Joe Moon from Boyle, Mississippi, about what it was like for a Chinese to grow up in the segregated Mississippi Delta from the 1940s to 1960s.[5] He wrote it in the form of a letter to a young niece that explained to her some of the difficult aspects of life for Chinese during his youth in the segregated Delta. I contacted Moon to learn more details about his experiences in the Delta. We exchanged many emails over several months in which he detailed and clarified the story of how his immigrant father, Jew Guey Moon, and several of his other male relatives came to settle in the Delta to operate grocery stores. He patiently explained details of grocery store operations as well as aspects of growing and picking cotton. Moon was also a rich source of information about other Chinese grocers, their working conditions, and the structure of the Delta Chinese community.

Connection With Henry Wong

After my talk on *Southern Fried Rice* in 2006 at the San Diego Chinese Historical Museum, I met Henry Wong from the San Fernando Valley who found my experiences in the South of great interest. He was eager to share with me the story of how his family came to operate grocery stores on the Arkansas side of the Mississippi River. He had come from Hong Kong at an early age in the 1940s to live in Arkansas for a few years where his older sister, Nellie, and her husband ran a grocery store in Round Pond, Arkansas.

At that time, I was not yet involved with writing about Chinese in the Mississippi River Delta area. Fortunately later when I was doing research for the book on the Mississippi Delta Chinese grocery stores on both sides of the river, I remembered my previous conversation with Wong and contacted him to obtain more details about his sister's life in the Delta.

He gladly provided me with a richly detailed account of how several Chinese families from all over the United States (Illinois, North Dakota, Colorado, and Massachusetts) came to operate grocery stores in the Arkansas delta. I found this information about these families to be invaluable to include in my book as an example of the vital role of chain migration for Delta Chinese.

When *Chopsticks in the Land of Cotton* was published in 2008, it helped alleviate a growing concern among Delta Chinese from grocery store backgrounds still living in the region. They realized the importance and urgency of recording and sharing their unique history. Over the past several decades, the number of Chinese who grew up working in grocery stores to help their families earn their living dwindled drastically due to the deaths of their parents, and relocation of peers to cities with large Chinese communities.

The few who remained began to assimilate and lose some of their Chinese identity. In the past several years, Chinese community leaders, realizing the decline of the Chinese population across the Delta, developed plans for historic preservation with a proposal for a _Mississippi Delta Chinese Heritage Museum_[6] to be housed at Delta State University. It already collected a new archive[7] of 21 oral histories from Delta Chinese in 2013.

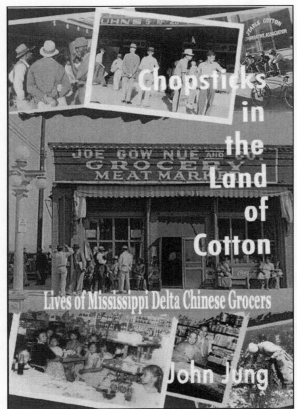

Chopsticks in the Land of Cotton cover.

In the same spirit of historic preservation, Paul Wong and the late Doris Ling Lee organized and edited recollections from Chinese who had attended the Chinese Mission School in Cleveland during the late 1930s and early 1940s during an era of racial segregation when Chinese were not admitted to white schools. The collection was published in August 2011 at Delta State University, with a book release and signing event that attracted many Chinese connected to the Delta - many coming from long distances, for the event.

Chopsticks in the Land of Cotton talk, Berkeley, 2008

The first opportunity I had to speak publicly about *Chopsticks in the Land of Cotton* after it was published in 2008 was at the Berkeley Chinese Community Church to their active Seniors group. It was my second visit, of what would become four, to speak to this cordial group but I was a bit anxious because about 10 retired Delta Chinese living in the San Francisco area came to the talk. If my presentation was not accurate, this group would certainly know. Fortunately, my talk passed muster as they wholeheartedly embraced it and complimented me!

Bay Area Delta Chinese after *Chopsticks in the Land of Cotton* talk, Berkeley.

A second visit to the Delta in 2011

This surge of interest in the history of Delta Chinese led to my invitation to the Delta to speak again, not only about Delta Chinese but those in other parts of the Deep South, with opportunities to give presentations at the University of Memphis, the University of Mississippi, and Delta State University. Frieda Quon, who was instrumental in having me make my visit to the Delta in 2008, was again the person who made arrangements for this return visit in 2011.

Talks at the Confucius Institute, University of Memphis

Quon arranged with Riki Jackson of The Confucius Institute at the University of Memphis for me to give a talk about the history of Chinese in the Deep South. Funded by the Chinese government, the Confucius Institute provides native speakers of Mandarin and other resources for Chinese language instruction to public schools. Many other universities in the U. S. and other countries have similar programs.

I gave my talk to a general audience of University of Memphis students and faculty interested in why Chinese came to settle in Mississippi and Georgia, how they earned their living, and how they were treated in the segregated South. I got to meet and generate interest among Chinese in the university as well as in the community, both those with roots in Taiwan and the southern Chinese province of Guangdong.

The following evening I met students in an Honors Program. I spoke about *Southern Fried Rice*. Students in this program, mostly non-Chinese, were open to learning about how Chinese immigrants like my parents were treated in America, a topic they had not learned about in their American history classes.

Fifth grade history books left out the Chinese

At the last minute, I received a surprise request from The Confucius Institute. Would I speak on Chinese in the South to a fifth grade class at the Campus School of the University of

Memphis? My initial reaction was one of sheer panic. I had spoken about Chinese American history to adults, seniors, and college students, but never to elementary school students. Would I be able to hold their attention? How could I make the material relevant and meaningful to such a young audience? I thought of trying to get out of the invitation, but upon reflection, I realized I had a golden opportunity. Why should fifth graders not learn about an important aspect of American history that their textbooks ignored? My only concern was whether I could develop a presentation that would be effective with fifth graders. I welcomed the challenge, and spoke to them using the theme, *What you should know about the Chinese in America that your history book left out!*

What is this statue a symbol of?

"Give me your tired, your poor,
Your huddled masses yearning to breathe free,
The wretched refuse of your teeming shore.
Send these, the homeless, tempest-tossed to me,
I lift my lamp beside the golden door!"
Emma Lazarus, 1883

Teaching Chinese American history to 5th graders in Memphis.

I figured I needed to start out with something to grab their attention immediately, and hope that I could get them actively engaged. I started with an image of the Statue of Liberty as I recited Emma Lazarus' classic poem that starts with the line, "Give me your tired, your poor, your huddled masses yearning to be free." Lady Liberty extended a welcome to the European immigrants arriving at Ellis Island in New York. The kids in the class were excited when they recognized it.

Then, in contrast, I showed them a picture of Angel Island and its Immigration Center, which none of them knew about. This is where all Chinese, and other Asian immigrants from 1910 to 1940 received a much less friendly reception than Europeans arriving at Ellis Island. I then proceeded to tell them the story of how the Chinese immigrants were detained at Angel Island when they arrived at San Francisco. They were treated poorly, housed in crowded barracks, and interrogated at length about their identities and family connections.

How effective was my presentation in promoting the students' understanding of the plight of the Chinese immigrants, why they were excluded, and how such treatment adversely affected Chinese in America for several generations? I was pleased with the attentiveness and curiosity that these youngsters showed during my talk. Without a follow-up assessment, I'll never know, but I was pleasantly surprised with the questions during the Q&A.

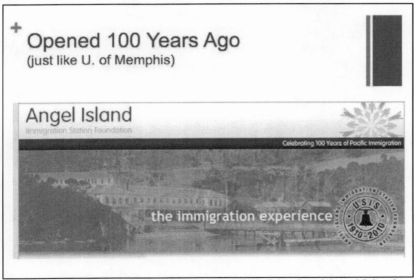

Contrasting the immigrant experience at Ellis Island and Angel Island.

Memphis fifth grade class history lesson on Chinese in America.

One boy was particularly interested in the example I showed of one of the many bittersweet poems that immigrants had carved on the wall while detained at the Angel Island Immigration Station. He wanted to know where he could read some of the other poems that were discovered by a park ranger when the barracks were about to be demolished years after the station was closed.

University talks

Frieda Quon arranged through Professor Kirsten Dellinger, Chair of The Sociology/Anthropology Department at the University of Mississippi in Oxford to invite me to give a talk, *On Being Chinese Where Everyone Else is Either Black or White*, about the experiences of Chinese living in the Deep South during the era of Jim Crow laws.

After the talk, I enjoyed Southern hospitality with delightful company of members of the Sociology Department and several Delta Chinese at the well-known Ajax Diner on the Oxford town square, which features delicious Southern food in an informal down-home atmosphere.

Finally, Quon organized an event for me with Dr. Albert Nylander before an audience at Delta State University during which he interviewed me about my experiences growing up in Georgia and the process involved in writing my memoir.

Publicity about my talks about contributions of the Chinese grocers to their Delta communities attracted the interest of Mississippi Public Radio, which produced a three-part broadcast of interviews by an award-winning journalist, Sandra Knispel of Mississippi Public Radio, with me, Quon and Luck Wing,[8] and then the next day with Harold Lum.[9]

My second visit to the Delta was rewarding for me, giving me a fuller understanding and appreciation of the uniquely challenging situation for the Chinese in the Delta, serving both blacks and whites in a strictly racially divided society. Their lives were markedly different from those of Chinese in other regions of the country, especially those in urban areas with Chinatowns that had many business, social, cultural, and religious organizations. Nonetheless, they maintained and adhered to many of the same cultural traditions, customs, and values of Chinese all across the country.

Beyond Black and White, Delta State University, Cleveland, MS, 2011.

Without the endorsement and encouragement of these network contacts in the Delta, it would not have been possible for me to receive these mutually beneficial speaking opportunities. The timing was also important as each year there are fewer of the grocery store families and their descendants living in the Delta. My talks there, and the eventual publication of *Chopsticks in the Land of Cotton*, helped stimulate more involvement and generate activity in recording and celebrating the rich history of the Mississippi Chinese, a unique Chinese community that despite being spread out across many miles in a rural area, managed to maintain a strong allegiance to Chinese traditions, culture, and values.

Using social media to promote Delta Chinese history

The realization that this close-knit community of descendants of pioneer Delta Chinese grocers was rapidly dwindling due to mortality, relocation, and the decline of economic opportunities in the Delta galvanized some of the Chinese still living there to work to create a historical museum and archives about the Delta Chinese grocers and their families.[10]

In 2010 I created a Facebook group page[11] for Delta Chinese to help increase contact and communication among the Delta Chinese who were now living in many other parts of the country. It was a limited success for a long time as few people posted memories, comments, or photographs. However, there has been a gradual increase in the number of posts and viewers and at last count, it had increased to 351 members. The page has served to connect people from the Delta, Chinese, and non-Chinese, including many who have lost contact over the years.

One exciting Facebook post involved a photograph of an elementary school class in Rosedale, Mississippi, for 1924. Linda Gatewood Bassie, a Delta resident, asked if anyone could identify the two Chinese girls in the lower left side of the photograph. It also appears there were three other Chinese students in the photograph. I could barely contain my excitement as I realized that a nugget of historical gold had just been unearthed. Rosedale was the site of the landmark school segregation case in which the daughters of Chinese grocer Jue Gong Lum were denied admission to a white school in 1924. An appeal to the Mississippi Supreme Court to reverse the decision was denied and the U. S. Supreme Court also upheld her exclusion (Gong Lum v. Rice, 1927).[12]

Although Berda was the older sister, the younger and more studious Martha was selected to be the plaintiff in the lawsuit. [13]

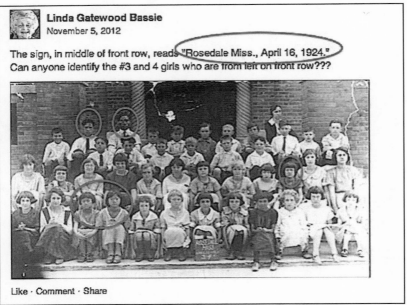

Linda Gatewood Bassie
November 5, 2012

The sign, in middle of front row, reads "Rosedale Miss., April 16, 1924." Can anyone identify the #3 and 4 girls who are from left on front row???

Like · Comment · Share

1924 Rosedale class. Lum sisters (front circle) and three other Chinese (circles).

Although the case has been widely cited, no photographs of the daughters, Berda and Martha, had been published to my knowledge. And, here right before me on Facebook, of all places, was a photograph of the Lum sisters in a class photograph taken at the Rosedale school in April before the local School Board decision in the fall that they could no longer attend the white school.

I had another extraordinary experience related to the Gong Lum case at the Cerritos, California, library during the Q&A following my presentation in 2009 about two of my books dealing with Chinese in the American South. A Chinese woman stood up, somewhat shyly, and proudly announced that the plaintiff, Martha Lum, in that historic case was her aunt! I was taken by complete surprise by this disclosure and did not think to get her name or contact information. I later regretted this failure because several times later I wanted to contact her for an interview. It was a golden opportunity lost.

Mississippi Delta Chinese website

Home page of Mississippi Delta Chinese <u>website</u>.

A limitation of Facebook for sharing information is that older postings are soon buried by newer ones so unless members read posts in a timely manner, they can easily miss some interesting ones. An alternative is to use a website where information is easier to access over long periods of time. I created such a website, <u>Mississippi Delta Chinese R Us</u>[14] where I posted historical background and current information about the Delta Chinese, rather than the type of posts that individuals typically make on Facebook about their personal interests and activities.

The evidence is only anecdotal, but it appears that the Facebook page and the website for the Delta Chinese have stimulated new as well as renewed interest and reconnections among Delta Chinese now living all over the country. I am gratified that social media and *Chopsticks in the Land of Cotton* helped the Delta Chinese realize the urgency of immediate actions to preserve the stories of the important contributions of the Chinese to the Delta that their forebears started. I feel privileged to have helped generate interest in the history of this once thriving Chinese community.

A book review of *Chopsticks in the Land of Cotton* commended it as an "excellent history" that "sets the record straight" by bringing attention to the overlooked Delta Chinese and their achievements:[15]

> Every child in America learns that the Chinese first came to this country to help build the railroads and then some of them stayed to open laundries and restaurants. But who ever heard of the Chinese grocery store owners of the Mississippi Delta, the earliest of which were established in the 1870s. Professor John Jung, author of several books in Chinese-American history has now set the record straight with his new book...not only an excellent history of these Chinese grocers but also a fine sociological study of conditions in the Mississippi Delta over a hundred year period.

In fall 2014, the Mississippi Delta Chinese Heritage Museum at Delta State University organized a *Reflections and Reunion* event that attracted many former Delta Chinese from across the country to join current Delta Chinese residents and their friends to celebrate their history and contributions. It was an honor to be invited as one of the speakers. The weekend event was a memorable and festive occasion for the over 200 participants that paid tribute to the achievements of the pioneering generations of Chinese in the Delta.[16]

Program for 2014 Delta Chinese *Reflections and Reunion* event.

Endnotes

[1] The timing couldn't have been better because my cousin Henry and his wife, Ronnie, from Atlanta were in town to visit their daughter, Jessica, who was attending nearby Occidental College. Another cousin, James, and his wife, Helen, originally from Atlanta also attended. UCLA psychology professor Ronald Gallimore, a close friend who had attended graduate school with me, came with his wife, Sharon. The event was like a small family gathering.

[2] James W. Loewen. "The Mississippi Chinese. Between Black and White." Second Edition. Prospect Hts., IL. Waveland Press, 1988. Robert Seto Quan, Lotus Among the Magnolias: The Mississippi Chinese. Jackson: The University of Mississippi Press. 1982.

[3] http://www.deltastate.edu/academics/libraries/university-archives-museum/guides-to-the-collections/oral-histories/chinese-oral-histories/

[4] Sam Sue. "Growing up in Mississippi." *Asian Americans. Oral Histories of First to Fourth Generation Americans from China, the Philippines, Japan. India, the Pacific Islands. Vietnam and Cambodia.* edited by Joann Faung Jean Lee (New York: The New Press. 1991) 3-9.

[5] Bobby Jo Moon. "Growing up in Mississippi in the 40's-60's." http://usads.ms11.net/bjm.html

[6] Mississippi Delta Chinese Heritage Museum. http://www.mdchm.org/

[7] Mississippi Delta Chinese Oral History Archive http://www.mdchm.org/items/browse?

[8] http://wknofm.org/post/chinese-immigrants-find-economic-and-social-mobility-mississippi

[9] http://wknofm.org/post/second-generation-chinese-immigrant-finds-opportunity-mississippi-delta

[10] http://www.deltastate.edu/academics/libraries/university-archives-museum/ms-delta-chinese-heritage/

[11] https://www.facebook.com/groups/msdeltachinese/

[12] https://www.academia.edu/440127/Gong_Lum_v._Rice_1927_Mississippi_School_Segregation_and_the_Delta_Chinese

[13] Sharon Lum, a niece of the daughters of Gong Lum, provided this information in an email, August 29, 2010.

[14] http://mississippideltachinese.webs.com

[15] Foster Stockwell. "An Unknown Chapter in Chinese American History." *Chinese American Forum*, 2010, 26, 2, 35-36.

[16] http://tinyurl.com/ngqndyk

5 Sweet and Sour

Sweet, sour, bitter, and pungent, all must be tasted.

My experience with Chinese restaurants has only been in the role of a diner, one who has had the pleasure of eating many delicious meals but has had no direct experience with what is involved in the operation of such restaurants. The thought of writing a book on Chinese restaurants is not one that I would have ever had on my own, just as I had had no plans to write a book about Mississippi Delta Chinese. But, as with that book, the suggestion and urging of a Chinese attending one of my talks is what started me on the path to writing about Chinese restaurants.

I previously described meeting Henry Wong at the San Diego Chinese Historical Museum at my talk on *Southern Fried Rice* in 2006, and how he became a valuable resource for the Mississippi Delta book because he had relatives who had operated grocery stores in Arkansas. Wong felt my work would be of interest to Chinese in the San Fernando Valley where he lived, and offered to try to get me invited to speak at his church in Northridge, California. Unfortunately, his initial attempts to persuade his church that the topic would be of interest to its members did not succeed. Undaunted, he persisted, and in late 2008 finally succeeded. My talk was about the Chinese in the South, for which I combined material from two books, *Chopsticks in the Land of Cotton* and *Southern Fried Rice*.

A talk when half the audience speaks only Chinese

Located just north of Los Angeles, Northridge is about an hour's drive from my home. Traffic was heavy as usual, and I just managed to arrive with about two minutes to spare. As I was catching my breath, the organizer advised me that about half of the audience could only understand Mandarin and asked if I would mind if someone translated my talk into Chinese for this part of the audience. Needless to say, this was an unexpected surprise, but what was I to do? I had no choice but to consent, but I wondered just how disruptive this procedure might be and whether I was going to survive this predicament.

Fortunately, the process was not as difficult as I first feared it would be. My translator waited until I spoke for about five or so minutes and then she paraphrased (I am guessing since my Chinese language skills are not that good) what I said. Mercifully, she condensed what I said into maybe two or three minutes rather than giving a word-for-word or thought-for-thought translation.

Once we got going, I adjusted to the pace, and found that while she was translating, I had more time to think about what I would say next! In retrospect, I am glad that I was told at the last moment rather than days in advance that a translator would be necessary, as that would have undoubtedly given me more time to develop anxiety thinking of all the things that could go wrong.

Surprise! This talk led to a fourth book

After my ordeal of giving my talk with a Chinese translator shadowing my comments, I was "rewarded" when my sponsor, Henry Wong, introduced me to a friend, William Lee. After lunch, Lee was quick in getting to the point, saying, "You have now written books on Chinese laundries and Chinese grocery stores. Now you should write one about Chinese restaurants." I was rather surprised, if not also amused, by his suggestion, given that I knew next to nothing about the operation of Chinese restaurants. I could not agree with his reasoning, because it takes a lot more than just having an interesting topic for one to be able to write a book about it. Lee tried to allay my concerns by offering his services as a consultant because his background included running three Chinese restaurants in the past, starting with a hole-in-the-wall place that offered only take-out food and progressing to a high-end restaurant in affluent West Los Angeles.

He ignored my reluctance to consider writing a book on Chinese restaurant history and asked if I would be free to have lunch with him the following week. I assumed this was not just a social invitation, but also an opportunity for him to try again to persuade me to tackle this project. I was right and, even though we had an amiable discussion at lunch, I realized that our ideas for a book differed. Whereas any interest I might have in writing a book about Chinese restaurants would lie in portraying the lives of Chinese running small family-run restaurants, I could see that Lee was more interested in a book about the larger restaurants that catered to the more affluent clientele. We did not have the same goals for a book on Chinese restaurant history so I felt any collaboration would not work. I politely noted I would get back to him if I decided to undertake this venture with him, allowing him to save face.

Yet, I realize that without Lee's suggestion, I would never have even considered writing a book on Chinese restaurant history. He planted the seed that led me to spend several months doing research and developing the concepts represented in my eventual book, *Sweet and Sour: Life in Chinese Family Restaurants*. It was eerie how ideas for my Delta Chinese grocers book, *Chopsticks in the Land of Cotton*, and my restaurant book both came out of the blue for me. Left to myself, I would have never considered writing either of them. It was only in response to the coaxing and prodding of others that I dared to investigate the two topics. Once I jumped in and started reading past research, I quickly became fascinated by the topics and eager to write the books.

A social history of Chinese family restaurants

Many aspects of Chinese restaurants could make for an interesting and worthwhile book. Most people would probably consider the culinary and gastronomic aspects of Chinese cuisine to be of primary appeal. A history of the kinds of dishes that were prepared and served, how they changed over time and place, and techniques and tips on how to prepare delicious food would find a large and hungry audience.

However, my primary interest in Chinese American history is the study of how earlier Chinese immigrants, despite the fierce racism they encountered for decades, managed to find economic niches in several forms of self-employment such as laundries and restaurants. A primary goal for my book was to include narratives of the daily lives of these pioneer Chinese who earned their living with small, often family-run, cafes and restaurants all across the country. Unless they were located in towns with a sizable Chinese population, their customers were mostly if not entirely non-Chinese. They served a menu consisting primarily of non-Chinese food along with a few American-Chinese inventions such as chop suey, chow mein, and egg rolls, and later expanded to include concoctions aimed at non-Chinese tastes and imaginations like crab Rangoon, General Tso's chicken, and sweet and sour dishes.

In my book, I wanted to describe what life was like for those who labored behind the kitchen door. What did the work involve and how did family members, including children, contribute to the enterprise? Since I had never worked in a Chinese restaurant, I was counting on finding and convincing a handful of people who grew up helping out in their family restaurant of the importance of sharing their personal stories. I wanted at least 10 people to write narratives of restaurant life, but they had to come from as many different regions of the country as possible so that I could see what similarities and differences might exist for the different locations. Aside from finding and persuading people to write, there was still the question of how well they could write concisely, and to the point. These were busy people and it was not possible to predict how long each individual would need or take to write their story, and, how well they would respond to suggestions for any revisions.

In finding these contributors, I was fortunate to have established many contacts during the writing and speaking associated with my first three books. Occasionally, I learned background information about my contacts that was irrelevant to my goals at that time, but which became highly relevant a year or two later.

For example, in 2005 when I was just entering the field of Chinese American history, I met Liz and Joe Chan at the *Branching Out the Banyan Tree Conference* in San Francisco that dealt with Chinese American history. I remembered that Joe came from a restaurant family in Fort Wayne, Indiana, so I invited him to share the story of his family restaurant in my book. He was very receptive to have the opportunity for "equal time" with Liz, who had contributed the story of her family's laundry to my laundry book!

Another contact from my research for *Chinese Laundries* was Bill Tong, a geologist in Chicago. I had previously emailed him after I stumbled upon his website on Chinese American history. In our exchanges, I learned of his family's restaurant background in Chicago, a fact that I recalled several years later when I began writing my restaurant history book. Tong was pleased when I asked him to provide the story about his restaurant experiences for my book.

A third contributor to my book was Flo Oy Wong, a Bay Area artist whose portfolio included some impressive work related to the experiences of Chinese immigrants at the Angel Island Immigration Detention Station, where from 1910 until it was closed in 1940, arriving immigrants from China were detained for processing.

Wong had previously contacted me in 2006 when she learned I was speaking in San Francisco about *Southern Fried Rice*. She was especially interested because her husband, Ed, had grown up in Augusta, Georgia, not too far from my hometown of Macon. She was unable to attend my talk but we met soon afterwards, and became friends and mutual admirers of our work on Chinese Americans. I learned that she and her siblings had grown up in Oakland, California, and helped with the work in their family's restaurant. I invited her to share her story in my book. She eagerly accepted the challenge and wrote about her family's restaurant, *Ai Joong Wah,* or Great China, and included some drawings she had made of the restaurant's interior many years ago.

An unexpected bonus from my friendship with Flo was that when her sister, Nellie Wong, an acclaimed feminist poet, learned of the planned book she offered to let me include some of her wonderful poems about her Chinese restaurant experiences. This was a wonderful and unexpected contribution!

My choice of a fourth prospect was Karen Tam, a talented young Chinese Canadian artist who grew up in her parents' Montreal Chinese restaurant. I wanted to not only invite her to write about her family restaurant but to get her permission to use images of her artistic renditions of dining spaces in family restaurants in the style common around the 1930s and 1940s on the cover of my book. The story of how I found Tam's artwork will be presented in some detail shortly.

I gained two more stories when I mentioned my restaurant history book plans to Mel Brown, an author who shared my interest in Chinese American history. Brown and I had become fast friends who had exchanged emails over several years. I finally had an opportunity to visit him and his wife, Lorraine, in their Austin home in 2008 after I gave a talk in Houston.

Lorraine came from Lodi, a small northern California town near Stockton, where her family had a restaurant. The Browns connected me with Lorraine's cousin, Julie Wong Hornsby, who lived near San Francisco and had a fuller knowledge of the operations of the *New Shanghai Restaurant*. Their grandfather began this Lodi family business in 1927, which Julie's parents eventually took over and operated until the early 1990s, and she was happy to share its story as part of my book.

Brown proved helpful in finding me another story about a Chinese cafe in San Antonio named *John L's*. He had been well acquainted with the owners, John Leung and his wife, Dora. Brown persuaded Dora, now a widow, to write the story for my book about their business, which operated for more than 50 years.

I still was searching for someone from a restaurant in the South, which proved to be difficult since there had not been many Chinese in that region. In 2008, I ran into Jasmine Kar Tang, a history graduate student at the University of Minnesota, at the Association for Asian American Studies conference in Chicago. We had met previously on a panel at an Asian American Studies conference in Atlanta. During a conversation, I inquired how she came to be interested in the history of Chinese in the South and discovered that she had grown up in Knoxville, Tennessee. I then commented that I had two cousins in Knoxville, Dominic Lo, who ran a restaurant, and Veronica Chang, who was a pharmacist. That comment really caught her attention as she exclaimed, "Oh that must be *Auntie Veronica*." Jasmine was not actually related to Veronica but regarded her as an auntie because she had grown up as a close friend of Veronica's daughter, Michelle.

Fast forward a year later when I was searching for a Chinese who grew up in a Chinese restaurant in the South, I contacted Tang, hoping she knew of one in Tennessee. Unfortunately she did not know anyone who grew up in a Chinese restaurant in the South. However, she mentioned that the parents of her boyfriend, Darren Lee, ran a restaurant in Chicago, and that he would likely be interested in contributing his story. So, my contact with Tang proved useful even if not in the way I first thought it would be. Instead of getting a story from her about a restaurant in the Deep South, I got one from the Midwest!

And so, without undue effort, coupled with some good luck, I was already hot on the trail of seven stories. However, I still needed stories from the South and the East Coast to feel I had adequately covered major regions of the country.

Since there were few Chinese in the South prior to the end of World War II, I figured it would be more difficult to find stories from people who grew up in a family restaurant, whereas I thought it would be fairly easy to find stories about Chinese family restaurants on the East Coast. I was lucky in one sense about the South because my research on the Delta Chinese grocers led me to discover the How Joy Restaurant in Greenville, Mississippi. But I was unlucky in that Raymond Wong, one of the sons of the owner, did not feel he could write an account without considerable assistance as he was recovering from a stroke that impaired his confidence in his writing ability. Fortunately, I had met his brother, Russell, at a talk I gave in Houston and he was more than willing to help put the story of the *How Joy Restaurant* together.

I got another unexpected break when I became acquainted with Chat Sue, a native of Greenville who was a retired university counselor from Pensacola, Florida. He had seen some of my posts on the Delta Chinese Facebook page and on the website I created for Delta Chinese grocer history. During the course of our exchanges on these sites, he learned about my difficulty finding a Chinese restaurant in the Southeast for my book. Fortunately, he happened to know P. C. Wu, a Chinese with a Savannah restaurant background. Wu, a city councilman in Pensacola, was excited to share the story of his mother's restaurant.

My final story, one about a New York Chinese family restaurant, came to me in another unlikely way. I had contacted my Delta friend Gilroy Chow, who I met during my visit to Mississippi in 2008, to inquire on behalf of noted Chinese cookbook author, Grace Young, about adaptations of Chinese cooking in the South that used regional ingredients. He and his wife, Sally, are accomplished cooks and even once gave a cooking demonstration of Chinese cuisine with a Southern twist at an event held on the National Mall in Washington.

When Chow discovered that I was now writing a book on Chinese family restaurants, he mentioned that his family had operated one in Manhattan as early as the 1930s. This was a pleasant surprise discovery. Who would have thought that I would locate a New York Chinese restaurant that was part of the family of someone I knew living in Clarksdale, Mississippi? I had made the faulty assumption that Chow had always lived in the Delta. He was delighted to have the opportunity to tell the story of his family's restaurant in New York. Now that I had 10 Chinese from family restaurant backgrounds representing a good cross section of regions who were willing to write accounts of their restaurant experiences, I was ready to proceed with writing the rest of the book.

How the Web led to the *Sweet and Sour* book cover

One day, even before I thought of writing a restaurant book, I stumbled upon a website[1] created by Bill and Sue-On Hillman of Brandon University in Manitoba, Canada, which included the story of the immigration of Sue-On's parents to Canada and details about the origins and operation of their family's Chinese restaurant in Manitoba. The site also showcased their musical talents and recordings of their band and Bill's voluminous material on Edgar Rice Burroughs, the creator of Tarzan.[2]

Among the many and varied treasures on this site was a section devoted to an art exhibit in Manitoba that featured art installations by the young Chinese Canadian artist Karen Tam from Montreal, who I mentioned earlier as a contributor of her family's restaurant story for *Sweet and Sour*.[3] Tam's wonderful museum installations faithfully reproduced the interior decor of dining rooms of Chinese family restaurants typical of an earlier period before World War II.

I was so impressed upon seeing photographs of her work on the website that I immediately emailed Tam to compliment her. In less than a few minutes, I received a gracious email reply from her thanking me for my compliment. Moreover, in her message she noted that at the moment she received my compliment she was in Syracuse in the kitchen of Amy Lau, my niece (actually my cousin's daughter).

This disclosure was startling but I quickly put two and two together, recalling that Karen and Amy had both attended the Art Institute of Chicago. So, what had happened was that Karen was visiting Amy at her house in Syracuse when she received my email. When Karen opened the email, she shared it immediately with Amy. When, to her surprise, Amy recognized me as the sender of the compliment, she then startled Karen by telling her that I was her "uncle." I was impressed how email communication can have such immediate and interesting effects!

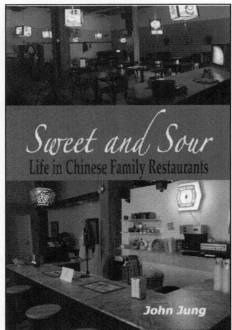

Sweet and Sour book cover with Karen Tam art images.

Tam's artistic installations of interiors of Chinese restaurants were so fitting for the topic of my book, *Sweet and Sour: Life in Chinese Family Restaurants,* that I soon realized that photographs of her creative efforts would be perfect artwork for my book's cover. She generously gave me permission to use two of her images on my cover.

Surprise! I discover relatives had a cafe in rural Canada

In my research on Chinese restaurants, I learned that across the Canadian prairies, virtually every small town had a small cafe run by a Chinese family, as vividly illustrated in a documentary by Tony Chan.[4] Even though they served mostly Western foods such as hamburgers, steak, pork chops, and apple pie, with the only dishes faintly related to Chinese food such as chop suey, chow mein, egg rolls, and egg foo young, they were considered "Chinese cafes" as the owners and operators were Chinese immigrants and their families.

One day I suddenly recalled that some of my relatives from China that our family had never met had immigrated to Canada more than 25 years ago. For many years, my mother received Christmas cards from a small Saskatchewan town where these relatives lived. As I recall, it was the family of a niece of my mother. However, I never heard any mention of what she or her husband did to earn a living. Could it possibly be that they were restaurant operators? If that was the case, I just had to find out because here I was writing a book on Chinese restaurants!

I searched through old letters that my mother had received over the years, but never discarded. I succeeded, much to my joy, in finding a Christmas card from the mid-1980s from a Quong family that lived in Norquay, Saskatchewan. Now it was 2012, and I was unsuccessful in getting information from the town as to whether there had been Chinese living there in the 1980s and if so whether any of them ran a restaurant. If there had been Chinese there in the past, they were no longer there, so my search was in vain.[5]

Then I got what seemed a lucky break. A few months later, I found a photograph on a website of a Chinese restaurant that I wanted to include in *Sweet and Sour*. I contacted Joan Champ, the

83

person who took this photo, and she readily consented to let me use it. Since the town where that restaurant was located was not too far from Norquay, I asked Champ if she had ever been to Norquay, in hopes that she might have known my mother's niece and family. Although she was not familiar with Norquay, she did know someone there and gave me his contact information.

With renewed hope of locating more information, I called this contact and explained the nature of my search. My hopes were dashed quickly when he told me he had only been in the area for a few years and could not confirm my hypothesis. Then he offered new hope when he mentioned that his wife had lived for many years in Norquay. It turned out that she had known the family and confirmed that they had indeed run a café. However, the parents were deceased and their children had all moved away. She did give me a telephone number of a Chinese restaurant in a neighboring town because she thought the owners knew my mother's niece.

Then began what seemed like an endless exercise in futility. I eventually made three more calls to different Chinese restaurants in different nearby towns. All were reluctant to give me much information initially, but when I switched to speaking Chinese, but not very fluently, they became more helpful. Each source would refer me to yet another Chinese restaurant owner in another town. I was getting warmer, but still was unsuccessful in locating any of the descendants of my mother's niece.

I was frustrated, and felt I should end my search. Then a month or two later, Joan Champ, the photographer mentioned earlier, contacted me again. Champ happened to be a history museum archivist and had studied old hotels in Saskatchewan, some of which had Chinese-operated cafes that she described on her blog. This background led her to take a strong interest in my quest. She took the initiative to search city directories in the area for people named Quong. She found several Quongs living in Regina and sent me their phone numbers.

I took a chance and called one of these leads, but the woman who answered my call was quite guarded and reticent to divulge any information to a stranger even though I explained my purpose and described the information I had from the old Christmas cards sent to my mother. With some coaxing, she finally admitted that she was the daughter of the family I had been searching for but did not give me much other information. A few weeks later she visited her brother in Calgary and told him about my call. He was more receptive and we had a nice conversation about our kinship. I was invited to call on another brother if I was ever in Vancouver. And although that seemed an unlikely possibility, as I live about 1,500 miles from there, it so happened that a year later I was in Vancouver to give a talk and was able to get together with his family for a delightful dinner.

Vancouver dinner with newfound relatives, Hui Cheng Hu, Zhu Ming Guan, Garmen, Mai Fong Eng, and Joe.

Some contributors speak at my book talks

In 2011, I arranged to give talks at three different venues in the San Francisco Bay Area, where several of the contributors to my book of stories of their restaurant life lived. The thought occurred to me that it would be wonderful if each might be willing to share the stage with me on one of my book talk and speak about their own experiences growing up and working in their families' restaurants.

Flo Oy Wong and I sign books, San Francisco Main Library, 2011.

Flo Oy Wong enthusiastically accepted my invitation several times. She spoke about her *Ai Joon Wah* family restaurant experiences at my book talk at the Main Library in San Francisco, the Foster City Library, and the Association of Chinese Cooking Teachers potluck gathering in Alameda.

Nellie Wong reads her poems at Omnivore Books, San Francisco.

Her sister, the previously mentioned poet Nellie Wong, read several of her poems about the *Ai Joon Wah* restaurant that she had contributed to my book at my presentation to the Northern California Culinary Society at the Omnivore Books on Food in San Francisco.

Julie Hornsby Wong came with her two young sons to speak about her memories of the New Shanghai restaurant of her grandfather in Lodi at my presentation to the Berkeley Chinese Community Church Seniors group.

Julie Wong Hornsby talks about New Shanghai Restaurant at my presentation, Berkeley Chinese Community Church Seniors, 2011.

When I spoke at the Chinese American Museum of Chicago, Bill Tong came to speak about his experiences in his parents' restaurant, Tong's Tea Garden, that his grandfather had started in Chicago.

With Bill Tong at the Chinese American Museum of Chicago.

The only reason I have not invited the other contributors yet to share the podium with me is that I have not had the opportunity so far to speak where they live. But if that situation ever arises, they will definitely be invited to tell their story.

Meeting Grace Young, Queen of Woks

One day around 2009 I received an email from a "Grace Young." I recognized the name, as I had a wonderful Chinese cookbook authored by Grace Young, but I knew that Grace Young is not an uncommon name. I wondered if this email was from cookbook writer Grace Young and, if so, why was she emailing me? It turns out that it was indeed *the* Grace Young, the one whose picture appears along with her mother and grandmother on the cover of her first Chinese cookbook, *Wisdom of the Chinese Kitchen.*

One of the many nice aspects of this cookbook was that it was more than a set of recipes. It was also like a family scrapbook full of memories, photos, and anecdotes covering three generations of women. The inclusion of recipes of many home style rather than banquet restaurant dishes appealed to me.

Back to why she contacted me. Young was preparing another cookbook and was in search of cooking techniques and recipes from Chinese who lived in the Deep South. She knew of my book on the Delta Chinese, *Chopsticks in the Land of Cotton,* and thought I might be helpful. I gave her the names of Gilroy and Sally Chow in Clarksdale as the best people to ask as they are accomplished cooks of Chinese dishes. On a visit to New York in 2010, Young and I got to meet in person for tea in an Italian coffeehouse in Chinatown. We had a too short but cordial conversation about our shared love of San Francisco, Chinese food, and Chinese history. I learned that one of my favorite San Francisco Chinese restaurants, Sun Hung Heung, had been her father's business for many years on Washington Street just below Grant Avenue.

Once word was out that *Sweet and Sour*, a book on Chinese restaurants had been published, interesting developments occurred. A foodie store, Kitchen Arts & Letters, in the upper Eastside of Manhattan ordered some of the first copies of the book because a customer asked for it.

Then Jacqueline Newman, editor of *Flavor and Fortune,* a respected and informative quarterly culinary guide to Chinese food ingredients, culture, history, and recipes called for a phone interview. She planned to publish a review of *Sweet and Sour,* but was not content to rely on just reading the book. Her unorthodox, but sensible, approach was to speak directly with authors about why they wrote their books and what their goals were before she wrote her reviews. Here is an excerpt of her lovely review of *Sweet and Sour.* [6]

The contents are fascinating, particularly about racial prejudice, and difficulties and lonely times for their owners. These owners faced many of these as they served a few Chinese dishes from Guangdong and many western ones, too; and, they served them to their mostly non-Chinese clientele.

Fast disappearing, their restaurants were small places now replaced by franchises, chains, and Chinese from other regions who serve different Chinese cuisines. This book, a memory-lane must-read volume, is about places and lives of the Chinese restaurant owners. It blends archival information, myriads of memories, and historical explorations about early Chinese family-owned family-operated restaurants, most in the south.

Learn about their harsh working conditions, savor the interviews, put yourself in those primary source statements, and see the pictures -- most never before seen. Glean contributions the many family members made. Garner the whys of their success. Get deep into the washing of dishes, wiping flatware and tabletops, even stir-frying chop suey and chow mein.

China Insight is a Minneapolis-based monthly newsletter published with the goal of promoting U.S.-China cultural and business harmony. It includes articles and book reviews on a wide array of topics including culture, government, education, lifestyle, and local Chinese events. In 2012, Raymond Lum, Western

Languages Librarian at the Harvard-Yenching Library, published a positive review of *Sweet and Sour*, portions of which follow: [7]

> "... an important historical survey that contributes significantly to the recorded realities of Chinese life in the United States. Many are the Chinese restaurants that no longer exist and that are known today only through old telephone books and business directories. No doubt families still have memories and hold documents on those businesses, but if no John Jung looks for them they will not be found... in writing this book, John Jung has rendered a great service to the faceless people behind the counter who deserve to be recognized."

Hyphen Magazine, which aims at the general public, publishes articles of Asian American interest, and interviewed me about Chinese restaurants in the Deep South for one of its articles. [8] I pointed out that growing up in the 1940s in Macon, where we were the only Chinese family, I never knew Chinese restaurants existed. The absence of Chinese restaurants at that time was not unusual for the Deep South. Until the early 20th century, the primary occupation for Chinese all over the country was in the laundry business because a restaurant required more capital, cooking skills, and the difficult task of attracting non-Chinese to an unfamiliar cuisine. The few Chinese American restaurateurs in the South adapted dishes to local tastes rather than serve authentic dishes because there were few, if any, Chinese patrons.

One other example of how *Sweet and Sour* gained some more exposure was when it attracted the interest of Chinese foodies Louisa Chu and Monica Eng, hosts of a Chicago WBEZ Public Radio podcast appropriately named *Chewing the Fat.* Eng discovered and read *Sweet and Sour* around Chinese New Year, 2014, and invited me to "chew the fat" about the book on their podcast.

Whereas the preceding opportunities to publicize my books were solicited by publishers and journalists, I also enjoyed a chance "interview" about my book on Chinese family restaurants that was later posted on YouTube. In December 2013, I was just "hanging out" with my friend Leland Wong, a prolific San Francisco Chinatown graphic artist and street scene photographer at a holiday bazaar, Kimochi Silver Bells. Somehow our conversation turned to the topic of Chinese restaurants and before I realized it Chris Fujimoto, a videographer, captured the essence of my views about the past, present, and future of Chinese family restaurants.[9]

John Jung

Author, SOUTHERN FRIED RICE: LIFE IN A CHINESE LAUNDRY IN THE DEEP SOUTH & SWEET & SOUR: LIFE IN CHINESE FAMILY RESTAURANTS

Hanging out with San Francisco Chinatown activist Leland Wong, 2013.

The sour side of Chinese restaurants

Most of the interest in Chinese restaurants has been on the culinary aspects, not surprisingly, since good food is in great demand. Even when Chinese were excluded from many occupations for much of the past century, restaurants were a major means for making a living. However, running a Chinese restaurant involved more than cooking skills and the creation of delicious food. As a business, it was a very difficult way to earn a living – with long hours, hard work, and low profits. Not all Chinese restaurants were financial successes, due to such factors as poor business skills, stiff competition, and economic conditions.

Sweet and Sour, a social history of the Chinese family restaurant, focuses on its positive or "sweet" impact on Chinese, although some discussion is presented on the "sour side" of Chinese restaurants. After publishing the book, I continued researching to better understand the Chinese restaurant as a business. I examined in more detail some of the difficulties in operations of Chinese restaurants and published a brief version of the findings in *Chinese American Forum*,[10] with the complete document available as a free downloadable online version.[11]

Endnotes

[1] http://www.hillmanweb.com/choy/701.html

[2] http://www.hillmanweb.com/

[3] http://www.hillmanweb.com/tam/

[4] Anthony Chan's 1985 documentary, *Chinese Cafes* in Rural Saskatchewan features Wayne Mah, the first Chinese mayor on the Canadian prairies, the Kook family in Outlook, Saskatchewan and the Tang family from Humboldt who reveal their views on race relations, gender roles, and small town rivalries. Townspeople give their views of the Chinese and their cafes. https://www.youtube.com/watch?v=ILPbvU3VbeE https://www.youtube.com/watch?v=HePpmGD0_bU

https://www.youtube.com/watch?v=g8R9ydzydoc

https://www.youtube.com/watch?v=glH915-wmuQ

[5] A former student, Sharon Sandomirksy, who grew up in Saskatchewan, confirmed everything I had read about small cafes run by Chinese in virtually every little town.

We went to a Chinese restaurant in Regina just about every Sunday named W. K. Chop Suey…it was full of Jewish people on Sundays!!! Sometimes after fishing we would take the fish to the restaurant. They would fast fry it and cover it with candied vegetables and chopped onions and peanuts. When we went to Calgary to visit relatives, we regularly went for Chinese food. In Regina, and I assume other western towns, instead of convenience stores, there were "Tea Rooms" that served Chinese food as well. When I was young I assumed that all small towns had at least one Chinese restaurant.

[6] http://www.flavorandfortune.com/dataaccess/book.php?reviewID=467

[7] Raymond Lum. Book review of John Jung, *Sweet and Sour: Life in Chinese Family Restaurants*. Yin and Yang Press, *2010*. China Insight, 2012. http://tinyurl.com/csmswvt

[8] http://www.hyphenmagazine.com/magazine/issue-26-south/behind-fried-rice-curtain-part-2

[9] https://www.youtube.com/watch?v=0Pktkjdyedo

[10] John Jung. "The Sour Side of Chinese Restaurants," *Chinese American Forum*, 2013, XXIX (1), 1-22.

[11] http://www.scribd.com/doc/156659481/The-Sour-Side-of-Chinese-Restaurants

6 One Event Leads to Another

My newfound "post-retirement career" in Chinese American history developed and grew as I connected, often by chance rather than planning, with many influential and knowledgeable people. So many experiences of this type occurred that, before long, nothing seemed to be beyond the possible. Here are a few examples to illustrate why I came to "expect the unexpected."

2006 OCA talk led to my 2010 National Archives talk

Little could I foresee back in 2006 when I spoke to the Organization of Chinese Americans (OCA) Chapter in Atlanta (described in Chapter 2) that my contacts there would indirectly lead to an invitation for me to be the Keynote Speaker in 2010 at the "We Are America: Asian Pacific Americans in the U. S. South" Symposium held at the Southeast National Archives in Morrow, Georgia.

This is how that came about. In late 2009 I was trying to find opportunities to speak about my forthcoming book, *Sweet and Sour*. I recalled how helpful Dennis and Teresa Chao, of the Atlanta chapter of the OCA, had been in arranging my talk with their organization in 2006. I made an inquiry to Teresa to see if the OCA might be interested in inviting me to speak again in Atlanta. She was now working in New York, but she connected me with Tricia Sung, who was new to the South, but very active in Asian Pacific American programs and activities.

The timing was fortuitous as she was a leader of the Friends of the National Archives Southeast, which was planning a symposium in May 2010 for the National Archives, focusing on Asian Pacific Americans in the South. Headlining the event were two leading Asian American Congressmen, Mike Honda, Democrat from California and Anh Joseph Cao, Republican from Louisiana, the first Vietnamese to be elected to Congress.[1] Sung invited me to participate as a keynote speaker on this impressive program.

The **Friends of the National Archives Southeast Region (FNAS)** in collaboration with Asian Pacific American community organizations and archival institutions proudly present the first celebration of Asian Pacific American Heritage Month at the National Archives at Atlanta:

We are America: Asian Pacific Americans in the US South

Saturday, May 1, 2010

10:00 – 1:00 (workshops from 2 – 3)

National Archives at Atlanta
5780 Jonesboro Road, Morrow, GA 30260

Congressional Asian Pacific American Caucus
Chairman, Congressman Mike Honda (D-CA)
Congressman Anh Joseph Cao (R-LA)

APA Southern History Lecture
Baoky Vu, Legacies of APAs in the South

FNAS APA Genealogical Keynote Lecture
John Jung, Professor Emeritus and Author

National Archives APA Specialist Lecture
Bill Greene, Archivist, National Archives-San Francisco

Asian Pacific American Heritage Month event. National Archives, Atlanta, 2010.

Given that the National Archives was the event sponsor, I decided to base my keynote on the immigration trials and ordeals that Chinese immigrants suffered when trying to enter the United States following the 1882 Chinese Exclusion Act.

In my talk, *Searching for Needles in Haystacks: Tracing Chinese Immigrants to America,* I told audience members how they might proceed in searching for the records of their own immigrant parents, using my own search for the immigration files of my parents as an example.

I was surprised, but delighted, that Jack Peng, editor of *Chinese American Forum*, a small quarterly journal published in Seattle that covers issues concerning U. S. relations with China and other topics relevant to Chinese Americans, noticed the talk and invited me to write a paper for publication based on my presentation.[2]

The growing interest in Chinese in the South led Peng to invite me in 2011 to write a second article, one dealing with the previously mentioned historic school segregation court case in Mississippi that challenged the denial of Chinese children to attend white schools. This policy was upheld at the state level in 1924. The challenge went to the U. S. Supreme Court, which also upheld Mississippi's school segregation law on the grounds that white schools were by law for Caucasians only, a policy that continued until the late 1940s, *Gong Lum v. Rice, 1927*.[3]

My talk on *Southern Fried Rice* in 2009 at the Chinese Historical Society of Southern California (CHSSC) led to several other talks in the area. Gordon Hom at the CHSSC connected me with the Torrance, California, library where I was invited to speak on *Sweet and Sour* in 2012 and on *Chopsticks in the Land of Cotton* in 2013. He also arranged a talk at the Monterey Park Library about Chinese in the American South, where I talked about both *Southern Fried Rice* and *Chopsticks in the Land of Cotton*.

Sweet and Sour book talk at Torrance, California, Library, 2012.

Three talks in Cerritos, California

At a 2009 talk at the Cerritos, California, Library by CHSSC Board Member Jenni Cho on her book about Chinatown, Los Angeles, I ran into William Lee, the person who had convinced me to write *Sweet and Sour*. He knew and introduced me to the librarian in charge of public lectures, Padmini Prabhakar. Lee suggested that she should invite me to speak about my books, which would be of interest to the large Chinese population in the Cerritos area. Consequently, I received not one, but eventually three, invitations to speak at what is arguably the most attractive public library auditorium anywhere.[4]

My several book talks in Southern California caught the attention of Linda Fernandes, head of the Asian Pacific Resource Center at the Rosemead Library. She invited me to speak twice in 2013, once on *Southern Fried Rice* and again on *Chinese Laundries*.

Rosemead, California, Library talk on *Southern Fried Rice,* 2013.

Foo's Ho Ho Restaurant Fundraiser, Vancouver, 2010

Elwin Xie, one of the contributors for my book on Chinese laundries, contacted me to see if I would participate in a fund-raising event in 2010 to support an historic and beloved Vancouver Chinese restaurant, *Foo's Ho Ho*, in the old and decaying historic Pender Street Chinatown that had fallen on hard times. *Foo's Ho Ho*, located in an area increasingly peopled by drug addicts, the homeless, and prostitutes, and threatened by the growth of new and larger restaurants in Richmond, like other Chinatown businesses, was in danger of closing.

At this event, the plan was for Xie, Judy Fong Bates, a Chinese Canadian author who also had a Chinese laundry background, and I to share stories about our childhood experiences in laundries at a fund-raising event aptly called, "Chinese Laundry Kids."

"Chinese Laundry Kids" benefit for Foo's Ho Ho Restaurant, Vancouver.

After enjoying a delicious dinner of Toishan village "soul food" dishes rather than the "faux" Chinese dishes concocted for the tourist trade, we each spoke about how the laundry was a central part of our childhood. I shared some personal memories of my life in Macon. In addition, since my Chinese restaurant book, *Sweet and Sour: Life in Chinese Family Restaurants* had just been published, and we were meeting in a Chinese restaurant, it was quite fitting that I also discussed parts of that social history.

CBC Radio *Chinese Laundry Kids* documentary

A totally unexpected outcome of this event was that it fueled the interest of one audience member, Yvonne Gall, a Canadian Broadcasting Company (CBC) radio producer, to consider doing a program on Chinese laundries. After the event, she asked if I would be willing to be interviewed in the fall for a radio documentary on Chinese laundries. In September 2010 she came to my home in Southern California to hold the interview. I thought it would be invaluable for her to visit a Chinese laundry. I checked with Chinese contacts that had lived in Los Angeles for many years and was fortunate to find one of the few Chinese laundries still in operation in the area and contacted them to arrange a visit. After Gall's interview with me, we visited one of the few fully functional Chinese laundries still in existence, Sam Sing Laundry in West Los Angeles, where she interviewed Albert Wong, a grandson of the original owner.

Sam Sing Laundry owner Albert Wong with Yvonne Gall, CBC radio.

Gall's hour-long radio documentary, *Chinese Laundries,*[5] for the Canadian Broadcasting Company aired in the spring of 2011 and included interviews with me and two other Chinese who had laundry backgrounds.

Crossroads Writers Conference and Literary Festival

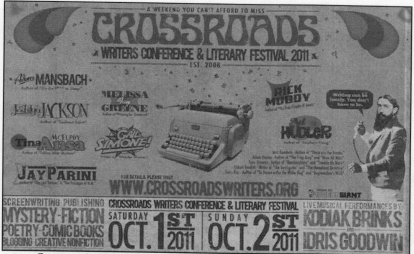

Crossroads Writers Conference and Literary Festival, Macon, 2011.

Another opportunity to visit to Macon was extended to me in 2011 that came as a total surprise. Organizers of a new annual Macon event, the Crossroads Literary Festival and Writers Conference, invited me to participate as a speaker. The goal of the event was to extend the interest in writers generated by the success of the 2006 Georgia Literary Event held in Macon. To be perfectly honest, I did not believe there would be very much interest in Macon in hearing about books on Chinese American history in the South, or possibly most other places for that matter. Fiction - such as mysteries, romance novels, and contemporary genres rather than nonfiction - was the main focus of interest for this audience, consisting primarily of college students and young adults with aspirations to become fiction writers.

Still, I could not resist the opportunity and the honor, so I accepted. My low expectations were fulfilled. At one of the three sessions I participated in, only my best friend and host from grammar school mentioned earlier, Richard Harris, and one other person showed up. Nonetheless, it was emotionally satisfying to talk about our family's history in Macon at a site just a few blocks from where we had worked and lived.

There was a better turnout for a panel discussion on "Creative Nonfiction" of which I was a participant even though I felt the issue was rather abstract or philosophical. A noted literary scholar on Robert Frost, Jay Parini, was the main attraction on the panel. The most provocative issue raised was whether memoirs are factual or fictional. I took the view that all memoirs are subjective, but most are reasonably accurate as to facts but not necessarily as to feelings. Parini felt strongly to the contrary, arguing passionately that *all* memoirs were inherently fictional. Insofar as memoirs are not entirely accurate, I could agree but to call them "fiction" seemed, at least to me, somewhat hyperbolic!

With Robert Frost scholar Jay Parini and Southern humorist Ad Hudler.

On the following day I got to speak about *Southern Fried Rice*. I was disappointed but not surprised that only about a dozen people attended, but among them were two schoolmates from grammar school, which made it all worthwhile.

At the end, one man asked me how my brother George was doing. I was surprised by the question, but since I had described

George's learning disabilities in my book, I assumed he was just curious to know what happened to George. I answered that he is self-sufficient and lives alone in northern California. He then told me that he and George were in the first grade together, and that George was a rambunctious kid. One day George had accidentally punched him in the eye. I put two and two together, remembering that one day George came home with a note from the principal that he had been expelled for some unstated misconduct. So, I said, to the gentleman, "You must be the one that got George kicked out of school!" We had a nice chuckle. Who would have thought that over half a century later at one of my book talks, I would run into the guy who indirectly got my brother expelled from school!

With grammar school friends Marjorie Simmons and Richard Harris.

Talk at Emory University, Atlanta, 2011

My overall trip was still a success because I had hedged my bets. Realistically, I expected that the Macon talks would not attract many people. I decided to see if I could give a talk in Atlanta either just before or after my talk in Macon so that my trip to Georgia would be more productive. As experienced air travelers know, whether you are going to heaven or hell, you have to change planes in Atlanta. Thus my talk in Atlanta would incur no air travel expenses, and there were no lodging costs as my cousin in Atlanta offered me not only lodging but also the use of a car for my weekend trip to Macon where my best friend from grammar school invited me to stay at his house. All I had to pay for was gas from Atlanta to Macon and back!

Tricia Sung, who had previously invited me to speak in 2010 in Atlanta at an event held at the National Archives for the Asian Pacific American Historical Society, was very helpful in working with other groups such as the Atlanta Chapters of the Organization of Chinese Americans, the National Association of Chinese Americans, and the U.S. China Peoples Friendship Association (USCPFA) to co-sponsor my talk at Emory University, *Searching for his Chinese American Identity, A Psychologist Morphs into An Historian.* Sung also arranged for me to be interviewed by Steve Goss on his local NPR radio program about the meaning and significance of the concept of *paper sons* for Chinese immigrants.

Are there any future trips to Macon for me? I don't know, but if there are, they may turn up some other fascinating discoveries.

USCPFA National Seminar, Washington, 2012

My Atlanta talk went so well that it led USCPFA Atlanta Chapter President Peggy Roney to recommend to the organization's National President, Diana Greer, that she invite me to speak at the 2012 USCPFA National Seminar to be held in Washington the following April.

I was invited, but unfortunately, however, I would have to pay my own travel expenses, as the organization could not afford the cost of bringing me from California. Still, the opportunity to speak to such an important and different type of group from the audiences I was accustomed to was tempting. I asked whether the organization might not request a complimentary room from the

102

conference hotel, and was successful in getting a shared double room free for two nights.

I would still have to bear the costs of the airfare. The deciding factor for me was whether I could arrange a second talk to another organization during my D. C. visit. I hoped that by having a second venue where I might sell a few more books I might be able to recoup most, if not all, of my airfare!

It so happened that a few months earlier, Haipei Shue, President of the National Council of Chinese Americans, had contacted me because he wanted to join the Mississippi Delta Chinese Facebook page. He suggested that if I ever planned to be in the D. C. area, there would be interest in having me speak. At that time, I did not foresee such a trip anytime soon. However, now that I was thinking of going to Washington to speak at the USCPFA meeting, I contacted Shue to see if his organization would sponsor me for a talk during the same week. Combined with the support of Stan Lou at the D. C. Chapter of the OCA, and Ted Gong at the C.A.C.A. Washington lodge, I was invited to give a talk in Chinatown on the day after the USCPFA seminar.

With Ambassador Zhang Yesui at Chinese Embassy reception, Washington.

My talk, *How U.S.-China Relations Affect the Lives of Chinese in America,* at the USCPFA national seminar received compliments from the attendees. I learned much valuable information from other seminar speakers on important topics on their program. Meeting attendees from USCPFA chapters from across the country created new contacts.

The USCPFA seminar participants toured the spectacular new Chinese Embassy, where a reception was held in their honor. I had an opportunity to meet China's Ambassador Zhang Yesui and present him with a set of all four Yin and Yang Press books, which he graciously accepted, expressing the view that it is important that China know more about the history of Chinese in America. My talk at the Chinese Community Cultural Center in Chinatown, *The Value of Learning and Teaching the History of Chinese in America That School Books Left Out,* was well received by the audience of more than 40 that included two friends of my sister Mary.[6]

My Talk in Chinatown, Washington, D. C. 2012.

The visit to Washington proved to be a great success. The adage, "nothing ventured, nothing gained," applies to my decision to travel at my own expense to speak in Washington. I took the risk of funding my own travel with the hope that I could at least break-even with proceeds from book sales, which I did manage to achieve. I was willing to accept a small profit or even suffer a financial loss in return for the opportunity to publicize my books. My reward was the chance to present my ideas to new audiences and the opportunity to make some valuable new contacts among the USCPFA seminar attendees and from the Washington Chinese community.

RTHK documentary on Overseas Chinese History

In early spring of 2012, Annie Yau, a producer with Radio Television Hong Kong (RTHK) sent me an email describing RTHK plans to shoot a five-part documentary on the history of Overseas Chinese. She was the producer of the episode that centered on Chinese laundries and restaurants and wanted to interview me about my experiences growing up in a Chinese laundry in the American South.

This was a fantastic unsolicited opportunity that could greatly expand the audience for my work, since it would be viewed in many parts of China. The offer came out of the blue. How did I manage to be selected as a consultant for this documentary? I never inquired, but I can only surmise that press coverage of my four books, numerous book talks, interviews, websites, and posts on social media and blogs about Chinese American history elevated my presence on the Web. *Chinese Laundries* and *Sweet and Sour*, my books on Chinese laundries and restaurants, respectively were the most recent books on the very topics she wanted to cover. She felt that my background and contacts would also be helpful in arranging interviews with other Chinese with knowledge of Chinese laundries and restaurants.

It was encouraging to see that Hong Kong media recognized the value of producing more programs for their audiences about the lives of their ancestors who left Guangdong for North America in search of work opportunities on Gold Mountain.

Yau came from Hong Kong to Los Angeles in March 2012 on an exploratory mission to plan for the documentary and I took her to visit several small family-run Chinese restaurants and to the Sam Sing Laundry in West Los Angeles, where I had taken Yvonne Gall of CBC Radio a year earlier. Yau next went on visits to other sites and people, some of which I helped arrange, in Chicago and Toronto.

In April, Yau finalized the itinerary for her return for filming. She and her film crew wanted to come in early May to interview me in my home. However, there was a conflict with my schedule because around that date I was scheduled to speak in Portland, Oregon, about *Sweet and Sour*. The invitation for this talk had been arranged earlier through the help of Bruce Wong, a cousin of Paul Wong who had helped me with my Delta Chinese research for my earlier book, *Chopsticks in the Land of Cotton*. Bruce, who headed the Portland Chinese Student Scholarship Foundation, felt I could help draw a large audience for their annual spring fund-raising drive.

Book signing at talk on *Sweet and Sour*, Portland, Oregon, 2012.

Although I knew this organization could not provide any travel funds, I felt the cause was worthwhile. Moreover, my trip for the talk would also afford me with a visit to see my niece, Liz, her husband Mark, and her two college-age kids, Lauren (who designed covers for two of my books) and Aidan. Being able to stay at their house, and hoping to sell enough books to pay for my airfare (which I did), I looked at the trip as a family reunion as well as a book promotion.

Yau adjusted her filming schedule after confirming with me that RTHK could come to Portland to film parts of my talk on Chinese restaurant history. During the Portland visit, they also filmed part of their interview with me about my experiences in the Deep South, and then finished it the following week in my home in California. Finally, we went to the Sam Sing Laundry where they interviewed me in conversation with Jon Wong, the retired owner, about its history and operations.

Much of narration in the RTHK video is in Chinese, but most of the interviewees speak in English about their experiences in these family-run businesses. It also has segments filmed in laundries and restaurants in Milwaukee, Los Angeles, Toronto, and Brockville, Canada. The episode was broadcast in Hong Kong, and can be viewed online with either a Chinese[7] or English[8] voiceover.

In addition, Yau wanted to interview me together with long-time Portland resident and Chinatown leader, Bruce Wong, grandson of a Portland Chinese restaurateur who started the popular, but now closed, Hung Far Low Restaurant, back in the 1920s.[9]

Thanks to Fred Chin, owner of the Canton Grill, RTHK was able to use this long-standing restaurant, which opened back in the 1940s, to film Bruce and me the day after my talk conversing while eating, what else, but chop suey! First, the two-man camera crew invaded the kitchen for more than an hour to film the preparation of several iconic American-Chinese dishes, chop suey, egg foo young, and chow mein. Then, seated in a booth in the dining room, we sampled the dishes as we conversed about the background of these dishes that were very popular with non-Chinese customers.

Being part of the documentary was a fascinating experience because I learned about the complexity and challenge of creating a coherent, authoritative, and yet interest-holding film. I did not realize how many "retakes" would be needed, and how much time is involved for the shoot, much less the time needed for the editing later. When I saw the completed documentary, I was glad that such highly talented professionals were involved in producing it. For example, their state of the art computer animation of old posters and newspaper cartoons showing racist treatment of Chinese greatly increased the emotional impact of those images.

RTHK filming at the Canton Grill, Portland, Oregon, 2012.

KBOO-FM interview

During my visit in Portland, Andrew Yeh, of, arranged time to interview me on a public radio podcast devoted to Asian Pacific topics called APA Compass.[10] He wanted to know the background that led me to write *Southern Fried Rice* and how I developed a retirement career in writing and speaking about my books on the history of Chinese in America who worked in family-operated laundry, restaurant, and grocery store businesses.

RTHK Interviews in Southern California

A week later RTHK came to southern California to interview me about Chinese laundry history. I took Annie Yau and the RTHK crew to West Los Angeles to introduce them to Jon and Albert Wong, father and son, owners of the Sam Sing Laundry, the same laundry used in the CBC Radio documentary in 2011. It is one of the few full service Chinese laundries still in business and operated by family members.

Scene from RTHK interview in my home on Chinese laundries and restaurants.

RTHK crew prepare to film at Sam Sing Laundry in Los Angeles.

Jon Wong, retired owner of Sam Sing Laundry.

Chinese American Heritage Societies Conference

Another person I met in Vancouver at the *Foo's Ho Ho* event in 2012 was Judy Lam Maxwell, an active promoter of Chinese Canadian history. About two years later, she contacted me to invite me to speak at the Chinese American Heritage Societies Conference, in Seattle in April 2013.

Speaking at Chinese American Heritage Societies, Seattle, 2013.

My presentation, *Why and How A Retired Psychology Professor Became An Historian of Chinese America*, gave an overview of my "retirement" venture into researching, writing, and speaking on my four books on major aspects of the earlier Chinese immigrants working in laundries, restaurants, and grocery stores. I received many positive comments on the talk. I got to meet several writers, researchers, and activists that I knew by reputation but had not met before in person.

This set of interconnected talks illustrates how participation at one event can generate unforeseen additional opportunities. From my participation at the Foo's Ho Ho event, two unexpected subsequent speaking opportunities arose. When I chose to accept Xie's invitation to come to Vancouver at my own expense to speak at Foo's Ho Ho, I did so because the event sounded interesting and the goal worthwhile and with no expectations that it might lead to other speaking invitations. However, thus far, it has led to two additional worthwhile events, and who knows whether it might not lead to even more opportunities in the future?

Return to Portland, 2013

The following spring Bruce Wong invited me back to Portland to speak about my book on the history of Chinese laundries, which were an important part of Portland's early Chinese history.

Portland Talk At Graduation Dinner for Chinese High School Students

The next evening I addressed the Portland Chinese high school graduating seniors at a Chinese banquet. I was pleased that the audience of 90 grads and their parents - a total of more than 200 people - was my largest audience ever, and judging from the compliments I received from many parents and students after dinner they found my talk, *Being Chinese in America: From Anna May Wong to Linsanity,* was valuable in showing how far Chinese have advanced in society but that there is more to be done!

USCPFA Conferences

My previous successful presentations to the U. S. China Peoples Friendship Association in Long Beach, Atlanta, and Washington led to an invitation to speak at the Western Region Conference of the organization. The meeting was held in San Gabriel in Southern California, which relieved me of arduous travel by air, especially with the task of transporting copies of my books.

I was asked to speak about one or more of my books on earlier Chinese immigrant forms of self-employment such as laundries, restaurants, and grocery stores. However, I viewed this organization as one where I should develop a different topic. I wanted to challenge myself and move away from the comfort zone that I had developed from giving numerous talks about my four books.

Inasmuch as the USCPFA is concerned with broad issues related to U. S.-China relations, and many of the members are not Chinese, although extremely knowledgeable about China, I chose to discuss the diversity of Chinese in America and its implications. Prior to the mid-20th century, most Chinese immigrants came from Guangdong province in southern China near Canton, now known as Guangzhou. They came as sojourners who, out of economic necessity, left home to find work to earn money to send back to their impoverished families. However, they intended to eventually return to China rather than settle permanently here. For many reasons, many beyond their control, they did not return but raised families here. They, and their children, endured harsh lives, racial prejudice and even violence for decades before achieving better acceptance and success.

2012 Western Regional Conference
US China Peoples Friendship Association

- Former California State University Professor and author, **John Jung**, who will discuss the history of Chinese immigration in the U.S. and their family-run businesses.

- Author **Michelle Loyalka** –Discusses her book, "Eating Bitterness," – stories from the front lines of China's Great Urban Migration.

- The Executive Director of The University of Southern California's US-China Institute, **Clayton Dube** will focus on the economic and political changes in China since 1900 … and, its wide-reaching effects.

Shown above are John Jung, Clayton Dube and Michelle Loyalka.

USCPFA Western Region Conference, San Gabriel, 2012.

The Changing Face of Chinese in America

John Jung

Western Regional Conference
U. S.–China People's Friendship Association

San Gabriel, Ca.
October 27, 2012

The Changing Face of Chinese in America, USCPFA, San Gabriel.

In contrast, during the last half of the past century and continuing still, the primary source of Chinese immigrants was no longer Guangdong but places like Hong Kong, Taiwan, and the People's Republic of China, especially Fujian province, and Southeast Asia. Many of these groups, unlike the pioneers from

Guangdong, spoke Mandarin, and had some English fluency, professional skills, financial wealth, and retained residences in the country of origin as well as in the United States. To the non-Chinese, all Chinese in America are seen as one more or less homogenous group for many purposes. In reality, these subgroups with Chinese heritage are quite diverse and often indifferent to, if not at odds, with each other.

In my talk I wanted to direct attention to this "changing face" of Chinese in America and speculate on its consequences for Chinese among themselves as well as how it affects the relations between Chinese and the rest of America. One audience member, Claire Yeh, program chair of the Seal Beach International Friendship Association, invited me to present it to this organization. Its membership was mostly non-Chinese, unlike my typical audiences that are mostly, and sometimes, entirely Chinese. I welcomed the chance to speak to this group, as I believe it is important that I have opportunities to speak to more non-Chinese to increase their awareness of the history of Chinese in America so that I am not always "preaching to the choir." I was pleased that the audience had about 70 people.

During the evening, I experienced not one, but three, fascinating "small world" connections with some members of the audience. One woman, Julie Skaggs, who heard me speak in San Gabriel the previous October, had purchased a copy of my book about the Mississippi Delta Chinese as a gift for her Chinese friend in the Bay Area, not knowing that this friend was born in Mississippi. When she later related this story to me naming her friend, I realized that I also knew her friend, Nancy Bing Chew, as well as two of her siblings still in the Mississippi Delta.[11] Adding to the links among contacts, Skaggs invited Nancy's son, Cliff, to the talk.

At the event while I was signing a book for Mary Yuen she mentioned in passing that she was from Canada. To make small talk, I inquired, Vancouver? Toronto? No, she said she was from a place she was sure that no one has heard of, Outlook, Saskatchewan, a tiny town in a remote area. But believe it or not, I actually just happened to know about Outlook because I have seen a 1970s video of a small cafe run for decades in Outlook by a

Chinese, affectionately known to the townspeople as Noisy Jim. Needless to say, she was as amazed that I had heard of Outlook, as I was to be meeting a Chinese coming from there!

Another Chinese, Joan Eng, bought all four of my books. As we were chatting while I autographed the books, I inquired about her background. She grew up in Jacksonville, Florida, where her family, one of the two Chinese families in the area, had a farm where they raised Chinese vegetables.

Now it was a long shot, but I immediately remembered that my father would often order fresh Chinese vegetables like bok choy that were shipped overnight to us in Georgia from Jacksonville, Florida. When I mentioned this memory to Eng, describing the wooden slatted crates that the vegetables were delivered in by Railway Express, she confirmed that my description matched the procedure that their farm used. We were both surprised but amused as we suddenly realized that sometime back during the 1940s my parents must had been customers of her parents! So it was a very exciting evening for me to have these several "small world" experiences!

A second chance for an historical connection

In 2013 Carol Chen, the mayor of Cerritos, California, a Southern California town with a sizeable Asian American population, was the target of a vicious racist political ad by her opponent. I attended a press conference with others at a rally to support her protest against such tactics.

To my pleasant surprise, among those present at this rally was the Chinese woman mentioned in Chapter 4 who had identified herself after my talk in Cerritos several years earlier as the niece of Martha Lum, the plaintiff in the historic Mississippi school segregation case, *Gong Lum v. Rice, 1927*.

She came up to me and reintroduced herself. This time I made sure to learn her name, Candy Yee. It was providential that she and I were at this meeting. I was especially glad to have this second chance to meet her because, by coincidence, a writer in New York, Adrienne Berard, had recently called me for an interview because she was writing a book that centers around the Gong Lum case.

I was eager to tell Yee about the project of this writer as I thought Yee might have useful memories to disclose about both her aunt and her mother. As it turned out Yee already knew about the planned book as the author had already tracked her down and scheduled an interview with her in Cerritos. I was still pleased to have this second opportunity to meet someone connected with an important bit of the history of Chinese in Mississippi.

The Clothesline Muse

I was quite surprised and puzzled when I received an unlikely email request in 2013 for an interview from Lana Garland, a documentary producer in North Carolina. She was making a film about a significant but unrecognized aspect of African American history, that of black washerwomen. They performed laundry work as domestic servants or as independent businesses long before, and after, Chinese immigrants arrived and opened laundries in America. The film would capture an artistic theatrical performance about black washerwomen that involved dance, music, interactive video, and spoken words created by Nneena Freelon, a jazz singer with several Grammy nominations, with choreography by Kariamu Welsh and colorful tissue paper art created by Maya Freelon Asante to represent laundry drying on the clothesline.

With Lana Garland, documentarian for The Clothesline Muse.

I was fascinated by the concept of this work, *The Clothesline Muse*, but wondered why there was so much interest in interviewing me about Chinese laundries. Garland explained that, even though the focus of her film was on black washerwomen, she felt it was important to include information about Chinese laundries to see the larger societal context of laundry work.

Still rather uncertain about the potential contribution of my participation, I agreed to be filmed for an interview that Nneena would conduct in my Southern California home. I concluded that if Garland and Freelon were flying in from North Carolina for this session, it must be very important to them, but I did not expect them to bring a three-man film crew they hired from North Hollywood. Watching them take more than an hour setting up the lighting equipment and arranging the camera locations, I realized that I was dealing with some very professional people!

With Nneena Freelon, creator of *The Clothesline Muse.*

I pondered why I was selected for an interview for this project given I had no previous contact with Garland and Freelon. Apparently, they must have seen references to my two books, *Chinese Laundries* and *Southern Fried Rice*, possibly videos of my book talks on the topic, or even my blog posts on Chinese laundries. Without this presence on the Web, it would have been highly unlikely that they would have identified me as someone who could help them. Just as Annie Yau in Hong Kong probably used the Web to identify me as a good resource, Garland and Freelon may have found me in much the same way.

I was not sure whether they got useful information from me but I hoped that they felt my interview provided them with enough useful insights to have made their journey across the country worthwhile. I was greatly relieved when Garland sent me this message.

> Not only are you a gifted raconteur, but you also tell stories that connect communities, and tell you something about humanity. There's something about you that allows the Chinese American story to be universal. I can relate, empathize, sympathize, and identify with what you say. My greatest hope, as a filmmaker is to be able to do this.

It was a fascinating experience to compare how the task of washing clothes for a living by black washerwomen was similar, yet different, than its role for Chinese immigrants and that initially there was friction between these two groups.[12] I am looking forward to seeing *The Clothesline Muse* and the documentary on it.

More opportunities to speak in Atlanta

The Asian Pacific American Historical Society (APAHS), wanted to initiate a series of book discussions using a high-tech approach with Google Hangouts, which involves a "virtual discussion group" where an author can interact live with discussion group members with the use of webcams even though participants are located in different physical sites. Google records and posts the entire hangout session on *YouTube* for viewing by interested persons who were not available at the time of the actual interview.

Tricia Sung of APAHS invited me to participate in their first Google Hangout session in 2014. The moderator, David Kim, in Atlanta interviewed me about how I came to write *Southern Fried Rice* while I was seated in front of my webcam at home in Southern California and audience members were at different locations in Atlanta.[13]

Google Hangout for *Southern Fried Rice* with APAHS, 2014.

The following month I was physically present in Atlanta during Asian Pacific American Heritage month to speak at several events arranged by Sung. First, she invited me to be part of a program at the national corporate headquarters of Coca-Cola, which examined the prominent place that this iconic soft drink, which was created in Atlanta, held among Chinese in the South, especially among grocers. To provide a historical context, I gave Coca-Cola employees a brief overview of the immigration barriers Chinese immigrants faced.

Speaking at Coca-Cola Headquarters, Atlanta.

The next day I spoke at the National Archives in nearby Morrow. The title of my talk, *All I Knew about Chinese American History Is What My Mother Told Me*, was literally true. Since we were the only Chinese in Macon where I grew up in the 1940s, and school history books did not discuss the Chinese in America, my mother was my only source. In my talk, I reflected on the generational and cultural conflicts I had with my mother while growing up in the South that led me to doubt many of her accounts of the atrocious treatment that Chinese immigrants received. However, I acknowledged that I later discovered that she had not been exaggerating at all. This realization made me appreciate the difficult life that she and other Chinese had and why she made such great and persistent efforts to make me aware of the extreme racial prejudices that Chinese had faced, and which she felt I would also encounter.

Talk at Asian Pacific American Mothers and Grandmothers banquet.

In the evening, I spoke at a fund-raising dinner celebrating "Mothers and Grandmothers," a tribute to these important shapers of our Asian identity. I gave a keynote address, *Eating Bitterness: Lives of Early Chinese Immigrant Women in the Deep South*. Using anecdotes and photographs of eight Chinese women obtained from their relatives, I described the difficult lives of these Chinese immigrant women who endured cultural isolation and racial prejudice while also shouldering the burden of work in the family laundry, restaurant, or grocery store to support their families.

Endnotes

1 https://sites.google.com/site/apahmatlanta/services

2 http://www.scribd.com/doc/32807687/Searching-for-Needles-in-Haystacks-Tracing-Chinese-Immigrants-to-America

3 https://www.academia.edu/440127/Gong_Lum_v._Rice_1927_Mississippi_School_Segregation_and_the_Delta_Chinese

4 My frequent association with CHSSC led to my becoming a Board member in 2010.

5 http://www.cbc.ca/player/Radio/Ideas/ID/2179901268/

6 Two former students, Nicole Kang and Selma Caal, in the D. C. area attended.

7 http://www.youtube.com/watch?v=b0_w25052jQ&feature=relmfu

8 https://itunes.apple.com/gb/podcast/roots-old-new-stories-chinese/id641438491?mt=2

9 Although the iconic landmark neon sign was renovated and remounted in 2010 at it original location above the street level, the building is now occupied by a different restaurant. http://www.preservationnation.org/magazine/story-of-the-week/2010/whats-in-a-name.html

10 http://kboo.fm/node/37009

11 I discovered Nancy Bing Chew was also a friend of one of my long-time friends, Sheila Keppel, wife of fellow graduate student Geoffrey Keppel. I've known them for more than 50 years!

12 http://chineselaundry.wordpress.com/2014/03/31/washing-clothes-before-chinese-b-c/

13 http://www.youtube.com/watch?v=HjLR3quWkk0&feature=share&t=3m28s

7 Personal Connections Help

Knowing people and having friends with "connections" has been very helpful in obtaining many opportunities for me to speak to various organizations. Many of these linkages were due to good luck or being in the right place at the right time rather than to an organized campaign to secure speaking venues. Here are some individuals who were very effective facilitators in helping me get invited to several speaking events.

Frieda Quon

With Frieda Quon, Olive Branch, MS. 2014.

As described in Chapter 4 on the Mississippi Delta Chinese, the support and efforts of Frieda Quon proved invaluable in bringing me to the region to speak at numerous venues in 2008, again in 2011, and in 2014. She was born in the Delta to parents who had a grocery store in Greenville. Not only did she promote my visits, but she also chauffeured, fed, and housed me to make my stays as comfortable as possible. Since 2008, we have had many telephone conversations and emails discussing other ideas and means for promoting and preserving the history of the Delta Chinese. Quon has been a leader in the development of the recently established Mississippi Delta Chinese Heritage Museum at Delta State University.

Tricia Sung

With Tricia Sung at National Archives, Morrow, GA.

The primary mover and organizer for the Asian Pacific American Historical Society in Atlanta has been Tricia Sung who came to the South from New York only a few years ago. Through my contact with her, I received invitations to talk in Atlanta at the National Archives in 2010 and 2014, and at Emory University in 2011, as well as the previously mentioned event at Coca-Cola headquarters.

Sylvia Sun Minnick

With Sylvia Sun Minnick, Los Angeles, 2014.

One of my early supporters and mentors was Sylvia Sun Minnick in Stockton, California. Jean Bader, a colleague at California State University, Long Beach, suggested that I contact Minnick, her long-time friend, for advice when I mentioned my plans to write a memoir about growing up in Georgia. Bader noted that Sylvia was the author of *SamFow, The San Joaquin Chinese Legacy*, an excellent history of Chinese in the San Joaquin Valley, and would be interested in my story about Chinese in Georgia.

I did not follow up on this good advice for almost a year partly because I was reluctant to impose on someone I did not know. When I finally called Minnick, she was very helpful with pointed questions that helped me focus the direction of the memoir. Interestingly, I discovered that she and I had both attended Lowell High School in San Francisco and lived literally around the corner of Polk and Washington Streets from each other. How unlikely were these commonalities?

We bonded immediately and became very good friends. After the memoir was published, Minnick arranged for me to come to Stockton to speak about it in 2007 to the Chinese Cultural Society of Stockton. And, as an afterthought, she asked if I would be willing to stop by Hanford, California, on my drive north to speak there first since it was on the way north to Stockton. This was a wonderful opportunity because Hanford, largely unknown even to Chinese in California, once had a sizeable Chinese population of hundreds of Chinese laborers recruited for railroad construction. Decades later, around the 1960s Hanford became a Mecca for devotees of a new Chinese cuisine, which was more upscale than the prevalent Cantonese cuisine. Combining French and Chinese culinary concepts to create a cuisine called *Chinoise*, Richard Wing, a local son, had served as General George Marshall's personal cook during World War II. His sister-in-law, Camille Wing, was my wonderful hostess who gave me a personal tour of China Alley, where Wing's restaurant once thrived, attracting celebrities and dignitaries from far and wide.

After my talk in Stockton, I was fortunate to coordinate my travel schedule so that on my return drive to southern California I stopped in Salinas, another once-thriving center of Chinese immigrants, where I spoke to the Chinese American Citizens Alliance held at the Confucius Church.

Joe and Liz Chan

I met Joe and Liz Chan at the 2005 San Francisco *Branching Out The Banyan Tree* conference. I was walking toward the book exhibits where I noticed a man waving in my direction and gesturing for me to come speak with him. Joe Chan introduced himself, and a few moments later, his wife, Liz. If they seem familiar, it is because in Chapter 3. I described how Liz became a contributor to the *Chinese Laundries* book and in Chapter 5 how Joe became as a contributor to the *Sweet and Sour* book.

The Chans are retirees who volunteer as docents at the Angel Island Immigration Station in the San Francisco Bay. They offered to give me a tour if I ever came there. A few years later my wife, Phyllis, and I did take them up on the offer even though we were unable to enter the buildings, which were then being restored. Nonetheless the Chans gained access for us to walk around the beautiful grounds.

Joe Chan persuaded his aunt in Phoenix to get me invited to give a talk to the Desert Jade Women's Group. The Chans hosted me at their "snowbird" winter residence in Sun City where they go to get away from the colder clime of their home in Alameda. During my stay in Arizona, I was also invited to speak to some classes in the Asian American Studies program as well as to a general audience at Arizona State University.

But a week before I was scheduled to speak to Desert Jade, the event had to be moved back one week because a key member in the Chinese community had died. When I arrived for the rescheduled date, the Chans met me at the airport with news that someone else had died and that his funeral would be held on the same day as my talk. I realized there never is a convenient time for people to die, so I was philosophical and fatalistic about the timing of the funeral with my talk. However, as many of the mourners were interested in hearing the talk, the hour was moved back an hour to allow people time to get from the cemetery to where I was speaking. Despite this unexpected need for rescheduling, all went very well with the event and I felt that I had "dodged a bullet."

The connection I made in San Francisco in 2005 with the Chans has been wonderful. Not only did they each share a family story in one of my books about Chinese family businesses, but since we met in 2005 they have supported me with their presence at several of my talks in places as distant and varied as Atlanta, San Francisco, Phoenix, and Lake Havasu City, Arizona.

Lucy Wong Leonard

One of the contributors to my book *Chinese Laundries*, Lucy Wong Leonard, who wrote about her family's laundry experiences in Hawthorne, California, invited me to speak to her writers group in Lake Havasu, Arizona, in January 2008.[1] Whereas most of my audiences at that time consisted of older Chinese, the Lake Havasu City Writers Group was mostly "lo-fan" or Caucasian; this talk presented a challenge for me. Would I be able to get a non-Chinese audience involved in a talk about Chinese immigrant life? I decided to combine my presentation about the history of Chinese laundries with a tutorial on the print-on-demand approach to publishing and some authoring software so that these aspiring writers could take away valuable information for their own publishing ambitions. Judging from their responses, the event was a positive experience.

An unexpected surprise was the attendance of my friends, Joe and Liz Chan. They were spending the winter in their Sun City, Arizona, condo and had decided to drive over to surprise me at my talk. We enjoyed a delightful dinner later with Lucy Leonard and her husband, Bill, and my gracious hosts who invited us to stay in their home, Pat and Richard Agnew.

Joe Chan, Lucy Leonard Wong, and Liz Chan, Lake Havasu City, AZ. 2008.

Mel Brown

When I was writing *Southern Fried Rice*, I discovered on the Web a book with the intriguing title, *Chinese Heart of Texas: The San Antonio Community, 1875-1975* by Mel Brown. Through an exchange of emails and our books, Brown and I found that we shared many similar interests and goals in our writing. As mentioned in Chapter

6, Brown connected me with two people who shared the stories of their restaurants for my Chinese restaurant book. The support and encouragement I received from Brown, especially during the early stages of my Chinese history research, has been very helpful, and we have continued to discuss our writing projects since then. Interestingly, I later discovered that he and Bobby Joe Moon, one of my key contact persons for information and contacts for my book on the lives of Mississippi Chinese grocers have been close friends for decades. It is fascinating to learn about these interconnections among my contacts.

With Mel Brown, Austin, TX. 2008.

Chinese American Museum of Chicago, 2008

When I was writing Chinese Laundries, I stumbled upon a blog on Chinese American history by Bill Tong that led me to contact him about one of his interesting posts. From this exchange, I discovered that his uncle was a leader of the Chinese American Museum of Chicago. I was familiar with this venue because two close friends from graduate school, Ron Gallimore and Karen Vroegh, recommended that it would be a good venue for me to speak at. Tong's connections to the museum led to my contacting Soo Lon Moy at the museum, which led to an invitation to speak in 2008, and again in 2011.

In 2008, I spoke about my history of Chinese laundries. This venue was most appropriate since Chinese laundrymen all over Chicago were the interviewees for Paul Siu's *The Chinese Laundryman: A Study in Isolation,* the first and most definitive research on this important business among Chinese immigrants from the late 1800s until well past the middle of the following century. On a personal note, since I attended Northwestern University in nearby Evanston for my Ph.D., I felt a close personal connection to the city as well.

It was an honor to have the poem, *"Let Us Now Praise Chinese Laundrymen,"* that I wrote for my book, *Chinese Laundries: Tickets to Survival on Gold Mountain,* included as part of an exhibit at the Museum on Chinese laundries.

Let Us Now Praise Chinese Laundrymen

In search of Gold Mountain, you, your sons, and brothers came,
Some helped forge the rail that links the land from coast to coast,
Then, for problems not of your making, you were held to blame,
Racism denied you basic rights and liberties accorded to most,
You were taunted, assaulted, and then excluded from the land,
Undaunted, you persevered and worked long hours into the night,
Resourceful, you learned to survive by doing laundry by hand,
For many, apart years from wife and children was your plight,
You slaved, skimped, and saved to have money to send back,
Resilient, you endured hardships with a determined attitude,
Of courage, endurance, and determination, you did not lack,
For which your children, and theirs, owe you lasting gratitude.

John Jung, Chinese Laundries; Tickets to Survival on Gold Mountain

---

My tribute to Chinese laundrymen at Chinese American Museum of Chicago.

Most unfortunately, the museum suffered a major fire later that year that destroyed some important artifacts, including my poem, but in 2011 the museum reopened successfully, thanks to the dedicated volunteer staff that has labored long and hard to create a beautiful museum in the heart of Chinatown.

Hazel Wallace

I was invited in 2009 to give about my "retirement career" in Chinese American history to emeriti faculty from the College of Liberal Arts where I had taught for many years. I didn't think this audience, consisting mostly of non-Chinese, would be as interested in the factual details of my books as a Chinese audience would, so I decided to focus on tracing the events and processes, many unexpected and beyond my plans, that unfolded after I retired from teaching psychology.

California State University, Long Beach Emeritus Association talk.

In the audience was Hazel Wallace, a retired microbiologist from the Long Beach Department of Health and graduate of California State University, Long Beach. Wallace found my work of special interest so she also attended a talk I gave the following month at the Cerritos Public Library on *Chinese in the American South*. After the talk, she introduced herself as the President of the Long Beach Chapter of the U.S. - China Peoples Friendship Association (USCPFA), an organization that I was unfamiliar with then. She asked whether I would consider speaking to her organization sometime.

A year later, Wallace had an indirect role on one of my talks even though she did not attend. In December 2010, I spoke in Irvine, an affluent city in Orange County with a large population of Chinese and other Asians. I was surprised, disappointed, and even embarrassed at the very small turnout. Unfortunately, there had been little publicity or promotion of the event, so the attendance for this event in a city with a large Chinese population was very poor, with only about 10 people, and that included four psychology colleagues, two friends, and my wife. Needless to say, this occasion was a demoralizing low point.

At Irvine, California talk with wife Phyllis, center, and psychology colleagues from left, Hanh Nguyen, Chi-Ah Chun, Young Hee Cho, and Kim Vu.

After the talk, however, three audience members, Stanley Yon, Rosemary Thompson, and a third person, none of them Chinese, stayed to talk and ask questions. They were members of the Long Beach USCPFA chapter who came at the urging of Hazel Wallace, the aforementioned president of this group. Fortunately, they must have enjoyed the talk immensely because a few months later, I was invited by this organization to give a talk about *Sweet and Sour*, my Chinese restaurant history book, at their meeting in Long

Beach at, where else, but a Chinese restaurant named Forbidden City!

04.02.2011

With USCPFA Long Beach sponsors Stanley Yon and Hazel Wallace.

Unlike the abysmal turnout at the Irvine event, the audience filled the restaurant with the largest attendance that the USCPFA Long Beach chapter had ever attracted. This unexpected reversal of fortune from my disastrous Irvine experience made me feel like a Phoenix rising from the ashes.

The important lessons for me from these two experiences were not to be easily discouraged by setbacks or overconfident by successes because each event has its own set of conditions that can make or break it irrespective of how interesting your topic might be. Certainly the extent to which the organizers are effective promoters of an event is a critical factor, one that the speaker usually has little control over. Since that awful experience I have been more vigilant and assertive in checking if sponsors of my upcoming talks are publicizing the events.

That was not the end of the endorsements from my benefactor, Wallace, who was also a leader with the Friends of the Signal Hill Library. She had them invite me to speak there near the end of the year. That evening, however, started badly. It turned out that, due to some miscommunication or, rather lack of communication, no arrangements had been made to provide a projector and computer for presenting slides. I did not panic, and just resolved to make the best of it. Having been a professor for so many years, I felt confident that I could give a decent talk without visual aids although I knew that many of my images would greatly enhance the talk. Fortunately, at the last minute, an able technician jerry-rigged a connection between a laptop and a medium-sized LCD flat screen television! It was not an ideal solution, but it got the job done.

Wallace also endorsed me as one of the speakers for the 2012 USCPFA Western Region conference in San Gabriel, California and for a second talk to the USCPFA Long Beach chapter in 2014.

Houston Chinese Professional Club talk, 2008

I got to give a presentation about two of my books, *Chinese Laundries* and *Southern Fried Rice*, after a fine dinner at a Chinese restaurant. There were more than 140 attendees including many Mississippi Delta expatriates.[2]

I arranged for a pre-dinner gathering with former Delta Chinese now living in Houston because I was finalizing my book, *Chopsticks in the Land of Cotton*, a history of Chinese grocers in the Mississippi Delta. I got to meet many people in person with whom I had had many prior email and telephone conversations about the Delta Chinese, especially Bobby Joe Moon. My frequent communications with Moon led him to suggest to Philip Sun, president of the Chinese Professional Club of Houston that I would be a good speaker for their organization. Sun and his wife, Chen, both architects, provided lodging during my visit in the beautiful home they designed. To my surprise, during my visit I discovered that Phil was the brother of my mentor and good friend, historian Sylvia Sun Minnick, of Stockton.

Houston talk on *Chopsticks in the Land of Cotton*, 2009

The opportunity to talk in Houston about *Chopsticks in the Land of Cotton* was special because so many in the audience had

Delta roots. Some had lived and worked in the Delta for many years before retiring to Houston. It was wonderful to see many of the friends I had made from my Houston visit in the previous year and to make the acquaintance of others, including Raymond Douglas Chong, who has done some outstanding genealogical work and written many beautiful poems about his Hoi ping (Kaiping) roots in Guangdong from where his father immigrated to the U. S.

Chinese History Museum of Northern California, Marysville

Brian Tom, founder of the Chinese Museum of Northern California in Marysville, invited several authors of recent Chinese American history books to speak in February 2009 during the Bok Kai Festival that has for over 125 years honored the God of Water. This historic site, located at the foothills of the mountains, was a launching point from where Chinese and other miners headed for the Sierra Nevada gold fields, hoping to strike it rich during the Gold Rush days.

The two days of history talks in this festive atmosphere added to the enjoyable social and intellectual exchange between the audience and the authors. I spoke on what life was like for Chinese in the American South during the Jim Crow laws era on Saturday after the big parade, which climaxed with a double dragon dance. On Sunday, using my identity as a Chinese American as a case study, I illustrated how this important aspect of a person is not a fixed or invariant aspect but one that ebbs and flows over time. In my case, it depended partly on the ethnic diversity of areas where I lived over the years. I titled my talk, *"Am I Chinese or Am I Not Chinese? The Ebb and Flow of My Chinese American Identity."*

The annual festival ended on "Bomb Day" and we stepped outside to watch the ritual of "tossing of the bombs" or shooting firecrackers in the main intersection of old Chinatown. This tradition of the Bok Kai Festival is somewhat akin to the running of the bulls in Spain, but in this case crowds of young men jostle vigorously in the street to capture red rings containing lucky numbers that are propelled into the air from some of the hundreds of strings of ignited firecrackers.

Second Chicago talk, 2011

I was delighted to be invited to speak a second time in Chicago in June 2011. This time I gave a talk about my book, *Sweet and Sour: Life in Chinese Family Restaurants.* Chicago was a major site of these restaurants and I was fortunate to persuade two Chinese, Bill Tong and Darren Lee, who grew up helping their parents in their family restaurants, to contribute narratives of their experiences for the book. As noted in Chapter 5, I invited Tong, who lives in Chicago, to join me and tell the story of his family's restaurant.

Q&A Sweet and Sour talk, Chinese American Museum of Chicago.

Two talks in New England, 2013

My frequent posts about Chinese American history on Facebook pages devoted to Chinese American topics and on Scoop.it, a website where I curate two Chinese American history collections of material available on the Web, attracted the attention and interest of Professor Wing Kai-To at Bridgewater State University outside of Boston. He and the Chinese Historical Society of New England invited me to come and talk about my books in November 2013. One evening I spoke in Boston's historic

Chinatown about the social history of Chinese laundries. A day later I spoke about the history of Chinese family restaurants to an audience at Bridgewater State University.

Chinese laundries talk, Chinese Historical Society of New England, Boston.

Connections of my sisters

Both of my sisters, Jean (Eugenia) and Mary had lived in the San Francisco Bay area for decades and knew Chinese who were actively involved with community organizations. These contacts led to several invitations for presentations of my books to their groups.

Jean had attended the University of California and knew many Chinese still living in Berkeley area. They invited me to speak to the Berkeley Chinese Church Senior group about each of my four books on different occasions. They always gave me a warmest of welcomes. Many of the group members had grown up in family laundries or restaurants, or at least knew people who had those backgrounds, so they had a strong interest in my books and were eager to share their own experiences.

Jean also had several close friends from her college days living in the San Jose area who were active in a Chinese women's community organization, Chi Am Circle, which extended invitations to me to speak to their organization on two separate occasions.

My fourth book talk to the Berkeley Chinese Community Church Seniors, 2011.

After Foster City Library talk with sisters Mary Gee and Jean Oh.

My eldest sister, Mary, was also helpful in arranging venues. She lived in Foster City, California, for many years and persuaded Foster City librarian Cynthia Rider to invite me to speak on three separate occasions, 2008 (*Southern Fried Rice*), 2011 (*Sweet and Sour*), and 2011 (*Chopsticks in the Land of Cotton*).

After Mary moved from Foster City around 2012 to live in Chateau Cupertino, a senior residence community in Cupertino, she persuaded the director to invite me to give a talk about *Southern*

Fried Rice to an audience of about 40 residents. Since then, when I visit my sister, I have been asked twice by this group to speak again!

Chateau Cupertino senior residents attend my talk in Cupertino.

The importance of knowing the "right people" in getting opportunities cannot be underestimated. If I had to make "cold calls" on my own to arrange talks, I doubt I would have been very successful. The endorsement of an influential person is no guarantee, but it definitely increases the odds of success.

Endnotes

[1] Several years later I visited Lucy at her mother's home in Hawthorne, California, and was surprised when I met her niece who had been a student in one of my psychology classes.

[2] Among the attendees was one my best former students, Adriana Alcantara, a professor of neuropsychology at the University of Houston and her teenage daughter.

8 Chance Happens

Chance favors the prepared mind. Louis Pasteur

It never ceases to amaze me how many intriguing, improbable, informative, and even bizarre experiences I have had since I began writing my four books on Chinese American history and speaking about them around the country. These encounters have occurred at book signings as well as through emails. In many instances I discover coincidental linkages between people and events. In other cases, people shared useful and fascinating anecdotes and information about Chinese American history. I now "expect the unexpected." These experiences certainly enrich the life of this writer and provide more motivation to reach a larger audience.

Small world department: Delta Chinese

One reader of *Chopsticks in the Land of Cotton* wrote to tell me how much she appreciated learning more about what life was like for Chinese in the Delta because her aunt, who grew up there, had not talked much about her childhood in Mississippi with her. It turns out that I actually knew her aunt, the first and only Delta Chinese I knew until about ten years ago. She and I became acquainted when we attended the same university in the late 1950s.

Another improbable situation is that Betty Lee, a Chinese woman I have known for many years who lives just five houses down the street, taught elementary school for many years with this same woman from Mississippi. Furthermore, her husband John has an uncle, Hoover Lee, who lives in Louise, Mississippi, a small Delta town where he had once served as mayor.

And, it was completely by chance that I discovered these connections. One day when I engaged in some neighborly conversation with Betty, I mentioned I was researching Chinese in Mississippi. She responded by informing me about her husband's uncle in the Delta. This information led me to call John's uncle Hoover who provided some useful information about the Delta Chinese. About a year later I got to meet Hoover in person at a book talk I gave at Jackson State University, a historically black college in Mississippi.

Shortly after my visit to speak in the Delta in November 2008 I received an email from Pam Oldani, a Chinese woman in Illinois. She and her father had heard of my upcoming publication of *Chopsticks in the Land of Cotton* when they had come to Greenville for a funeral in September, which coincidentally was when I made my Delta visit. In her message, she wrote:

> I was interested in your Chinese Grocers in the Delta book that is coming out this year. Do you know when it will be available? I wanted to give it to my father for Christmas. My father grew up in Greenville, Mississippi in the 1920s to 1940s. His mother originally had a laundry and then a grocery store so he would be really interested in reading your book.

Her closing sentence was what really caught my attention. Learning that Oldani's grandmother had operated a laundry was an exciting and lucky discovery. Everyone in the Delta I had asked had told me that they had never known of any Chinese who operated laundries there, but my search of early census records showed there had been a few Chinese laundries in the Delta *prior* to 1920. But the only one after that time was the Hop Lee Laundry in Greenville at 122 Walnut Street in 1927, a block from the river and the prominent Joe Gow Nue grocery store.

I realized that I had just stumbled upon someone with a family connection to what was possibly the last Chinese laundry that existed in the Delta. I replied immediately to Oldani to request that she ask her father if his mother's laundry might not have been the Hop Lee Laundry that was in Greenville in 1927, and maybe longer.

In her reply Oldani reported that her grandmother indeed had operated the Hop Lee Laundry but later left that business to open a grocery store.

> My grandmother was Ho Shee Long and her store was called the Ho Shee Company, which was on the corner of Sidney and St. Charles Street. My Aunt and Uncle Ernest Chan also owed a grocery store called Sun Sing Company in Greenville which burned down after they had sold it.

I was more interested in the laundry that her grandmother operated so I asked Pam to see if her father knew whether her laundry closed after his mother left it, or whether some other Chinese continued to run it. In her reply, she noted that:

> He could not remember the name but it was down the road from the Joe Gow Nue store. He couldn't remember if they bought the laundry from someone or sold it to someone when they went into the grocery business. He was a very young boy at that time and couldn't remember. He did remember still being at the laundry in 1927 when the levee flooded but they left the laundry business and opened the grocery store shortly after that. My grandfather and grandmother owned the laundry but it was probably my grandmother doing all the work because my grandfather was a gambler and didn't help do much work.

> Shortly after they opened the grocery store, my grandfather died and my grandmother ran it by herself. She was a single woman raising 5 children on her own. She ran the grocery store by herself until she had a stroke. To me she was a pretty amazing woman to have done all that by her self.

He said his mother told him she got out of the laundry business that it was too much work so she quit and opened a grocery store.

These rich details that Oldani provided from her father confirmed my view that her grandmother operated the Hop Lee Laundry, quite possibly the last Chinese laundry in the Delta.

Stumbling into family differences of view

Another intriguing experience happened when I had just completed *Sweet and Sour*. My host at a birthday party, aware of my Chinese restaurant book, introduced me to a Chinese whose father had owned a restaurant in a large city back around the 1920s or earlier. Out of curiosity, I asked him for the name of the restaurant. I will not disclose the name to protect the identities of my informants but will say that the name was rather unusual for a Chinese restaurant. Moreover, it was precisely the same name of a restaurant operated in the same city by the grandfather of a young Chinese man I had previously met. My first thought was, could both of these two Chinese men be referring to the same restaurant? It seemed unlikely that within the same city, there would have been two restaurants with the same unusual name. Was it possible that by chance I had come in contact with two Chinese from different branches and generations of the same family! It would be such an unlikely possibility, but it seemed to be the case.

My dinner companion told me that his father and a brother had been partners in the restaurant, which was consistent with my hunch that my two informants were talking about the same restaurant. This brother would have been the grandfather of my younger informant. According to my dinner companion, when his father, the older brother, had to return to China for a visit, he entrusted the management of the restaurant to his brother. But when he returned from China, his brother refused to hand the restaurant back to him.

What was intriguing was that this account was exactly the opposite of what the younger man recalled about the earlier history of the restaurant. He had been told that it was his grandfather, the younger brother, who started the restaurant. I was in a quandary over my accidental discovery. I wondered whether my two sources knew each other and that they held opposing views about which brother, the father of one man or the grandfather of the other man, opened the restaurant.

A few months later, I received an email from the sister of the older Chinese. She wanted to know where I got my "misinformation" about the ownership of the restaurant. My only defense was that my account came from a man who was the grandson of her uncle, or the younger of the two disputing brothers. Each of these two sides of this family had its own view and I had no way to arbitrate the matter. I debated whether it would be productive to discuss the dispute with all parties. I decided it best not to risk stirring up bad feelings over the distant past.

Still, it is a fascinating story that I had stumbled upon. It was a chance meeting with a descendant from one branch of the family and my chance query about the restaurant name that led to my discovery of the conflict between the brothers. The story shows that, in addition to the substantial obstacles that Chinese immigrants had to deal with in a society that was hostile to them, they sometimes also had to face internal conflicts within their own families.[1]

My books reconnected me with long-lost friends

My books reconnected me with two Chinese I knew from Chinatown's Cameron House community center in San Francisco back in the 1950s, who I had lost touch with over the years. In the fall of 2011, I received a telephone call from Don Mar, a buddy from my high school days in San Francisco who I had not been in contact with for over 50 years. The way Mar happened to stumble upon me after half a century is rather intriguing as it stemmed from Amazon.com's use of artificial intelligence to promote book sales. Specifically, when you buy books from Amazon, their computer will generate from its database of your earlier purchases some "suggestions" of other books it "thinks" might be of interest to you. Some of its recommendations can be really off, showing that "artificial intelligence" is often more like "artificial stupidity." An absurd fictitious, as far as I am aware, example might be if I purchased books like "Wind in the Willows" and "Gone With the Wind," Amazon might recommend I buy books dealing with hurricanes in Florida. I have mixed feelings about these recommendations, but I must admit they have often been very helpful in guiding me to relevant books of which I was unaware. But back to how Amazon's artificial intelligence had an unintended positive outcome for me.

Mar had purchased a copy of James Loewen's *The Mississippi Chinese*, which led Amazon to recommend to him that he might like my book, *Southern Fried Rice*, because both books are about Chinese in the American South. When Mar realized that I was the author of Amazon's recommended book, he decided to track me down. It was a delightful surprise to hear from him. We had an enjoyable time comparing notes on what had happened to each of us during the past 50 years as well as reminiscing about our friendship in our younger days. I'm sure that Amazon never considered how its recommendations could have such unintended consequences!

My books also led to a low-tech method of reconnecting me with another old friend, Calvin Lum. Around 2009, Lum phoned me after he happened to see my name listed in a directory of Chinese American writers while browsing in a bookstore. Now, every time I visit San Francisco, we try to get together to catch up.

Two small world surprises at once

As a follow-up to getting reconnected with Don Mar, a few months later when I was in the Bay Area to speak in Foster City, I arranged for an in-person reunion with him in San Francisco. When I arrived at the restaurant, he surprised me by bringing Ed Sue, a former pastor in Chinatown and also a successful architect who was a role model for many Chinese American youth at the First Presbyterian Church and Cameron House. As with Mar, I had also not seen or heard about Ed in over 50 years. He had learned from Mar that I had become engaged in writing about Chinese American history so he asked if I might know Murray Lee, a historian of Chinese immigrants in San Diego. In fact, I had met

Lee when I had given talks about my books on three occasions at the San Diego Chinese Historical Museum where he is a curator. To my surprise, Ed then informed me that Murray's wife, Gladys, was his sister!

There was yet another link from the past from my connection with Mar. He was a longtime friend of D. G. Martin, a successful journalist in Chapel Hill, North Carolina. Mar told Martin about my memoir, which led him to interview me on his radio program, *Who's Talking,*[2] on WCHL-FM about my life in Macon, which he also used as the subject of one of his newspaper columns.[3] Martin told me he fondly recalled that Mar and I took him to lunch in Chinatown when he visited San Francisco over 50 years ago, although I had absolutely no recollection of the occasion. That connection from the past combined with the additional discovery that Martin was a cousin of Carey Pickard, one of my junior high school classmates in Macon, made for an incredible story of the interconnections of acquaintances.

But there is yet another improbable connection involved in this story. A few weeks after my radio interview with Martin, he ran into Johanna Jung Kramer, an acclaimed regional food book writer of the Raleigh-Durham-Chapel Hill triangle. She happens to be the daughter-in-law of James Jung, the retired chemistry professor from a Chinese laundry background in Kannapolis, North Carolina, who as mentioned in Chapter 2, phoned me after he had read *Southern Fried Rice* on the recommendation of a friend. Jung was startled to discover how similar our laundry experiences were after reading my memoir and e-mailed his four brothers to encourage them to read the book!

There are other similar small world encounters that I've enjoyed during my explorations of Chinese American history, but these several incidents should be enough to convince you that among Chinese of my generation there are fewer than the proverbial "six degrees of separation."

Many times, too numerous to detail here, my books helped reconnect me with friends and acquaintances that I had not been in touch with for several decades, and probably would never have located without some link through my books.[4]

Association for Asian American Studies connection

At the 2008 Association for Asian American Studies meeting in Chicago, I wanted to promote my first two books on Chinese American history, *Southern Fried Rice* and *Chinese Laundries*, but the cost of having an exhibit table was more than I could afford. I asked Steve Doi, a dedicated collector of Chinese history ephemera and used and often rare scholarly books, who has a booth at this conference each year, if he would let me leave some fliers for my books at his booth. Not only did he readily consent to doing this favor for me, but generously offered to allow me to leave a few copies of the actual books for possible sale.

I actually sold one or two books, which were more than I expected since my books were not "academic" or "theoretical" discourses that would appeal to many professors who attend these professional gatherings. But the most exciting experience came on the last day of the conference at the very last minute before the book exhibit room was to close. I was just standing outside in the corridor when Doi came searching for me to tell me that a professor at his booth was interested in and wanted to buy copies of both of my books. Greg Robinson, professor of Asian (Canadian and American) Studies at the University of Quebec in Montreal had noticed my books and considered them to have worthwhile content for his courses. That late-minute discovery certainly made my day!

I was not acquainted with Robinson's scholarly work but found out later that he was a prolific and leading scholar on Japanese American history, especially on the World War II internment of Japanese Americans. Since our chance meeting, Robinson has been a staunch supporter, friend, and mentor who encouraged me in my work, and generously contributed nice blurbs for two of my books, *Chopsticks in the Land of Cotton* and *Sweet and Sour*.

Facebook connections

A few years ago, I became acquainted with the fascinating research of Yvonne Foley who has dedicated years tracking descendants, who like herself, were of mixed racial heritage with

Chinese fathers and British mothers.[5] These Chinese men had been recruited to Liverpool from China to help man British ships during World War I. Following the end of the war they were abruptly and unceremoniously repatriated to China. Many had to leave behind wives, and children. Many of the children grew up never knowing their fathers.

Foley and I became acquainted through an exchange of emails about her research. When Foley mentioned that she and her husband, Charles, would be visiting San Francisco in November 2012, we arranged to meet in person as I also had plans to be there. I felt that some Chinese in San Francisco that I knew might welcome this opportunity to meet Foley, and learn about her research, so I arranged a "meet and greet" lunch get-together through Emily Onglatco, an active member of a Facebook group created by Chinatown graphic artist-photographer Leland Wong, "We Grew Up In San Francisco Chinatown," or simply, WGUISFCT.[6] By coincidence, David Wong, creator of an outstanding graphic novel on Chinese Canadian history, *Escape to Gold Mountain*, happened to be in the area the same weekend for a book signing. He learned about the meeting via Facebook and was interested in joining us, so now we had three scholars of Chinese immigrant history on board.

One of the tables of attendees at the WGUISFCT group meeting.

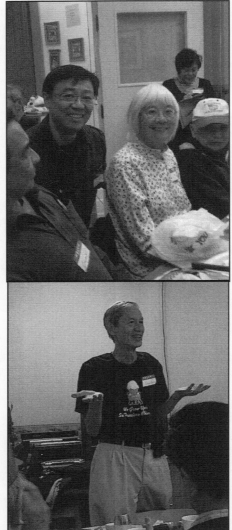

Top, David Wong, Judy Yung, and Eddie Fung. Bottom: John Jung.

The announcement of the meeting on Facebook led noted historian Judy Yung to join the group meeting along with her husband, the subject of her book, *The Adventures of Eddie Fung: Chinatown Kid, Texas Cowboy, Prisoner of War*. We had now gone from two to four scholars coming to the event that was attended by about 25 WGUISFCT members. There was lively conversation during lunch, and stimulating discussion of issues of interest to Chinese Americans for well over another hour. It is safe to say that a good time was had by all at this loosely planned get-together at the Pacific Court Cafe in Chinatown.

A tale of two Leland Wongs

The day before my San Francisco lunch with photographer Leland Wong and his WGUISFCT Facebook Group, my sister in Cupertino called me in Southern California to tell me she received an intriguing call from a Chinese man from near San Francisco. He had discovered that I had listed his father who operated a laundry in Chattanooga, Tennessee, around the 1930s to 1950s in my family tree chart in my book, *Chinese Laundries: Tickets to Survival on Gold Mountain*. His sister had purchased the book at one of my book talks and shown him my chart in Chapter 3 that identified the 19 male descendants of my great, great grandfather Fun Fai Loo that had operated laundries in the Deep South in the first half of the last century.

Believe it or not, this man's name, Leland Wong, was exactly the same as that of the creator of the WGUISFCT Facebook Group! The father of this *other* Leland Wong, Poy Wong, opened a laundromat in San Francisco in the early 1950s after retiring from laundry work in Chattanooga for many years just as my parents had done after closing their laundry in Georgia. Furthermore, both of these laundromats were located on Polk Street, only about six or seven blocks apart! It seemed highly unlikely that such parallels occurred.

Wong had to do some detective work to locate my sister and me. He had a friend, or perhaps relative, originally from Augusta, Georgia, who gave him the telephone number of June Loo, the widow of my father's cousin, Loo Heung Sec, who had a laundry in Augusta for many years. In turn, Loo gave him the telephone number of my sister Mary in northern California and he called her to find out how he could reach me so he could discuss details of his father's immigration history. The timing could not have been any better than if we had planned it because I was flying to San

Francisco that *very* day to meet with the other Leland Wong, the graphics artist and creator of WGUISFCT on Facebook.

I was preoccupied arranging details of my trip to San Francisco, so I did not ask for his name. When I actually met the Leland Wong who was my distant relative in person, I finally realized that his name was identical with that of the graphic artist Leland Wong. Since he did not know I was acquainted with the artist Leland Wong, this coincidence could easily have gone by undetected by him.

However, I just happened to be wearing an artistic T-shirt that artist Leland designed for the WGUISFCT group. Upon seeing and recognizing the shirt, he asked if, and how, I knew artist Leland. He then informed me that the two Leland Wongs were longtime acquaintances. In fact they had attended the same junior high school. Having the same name often posed problems. For example, their bank accounts, which happened to be at the same bank, had been a source of bookkeeping errors on more than one occasion.

Leland Wong shares family documents with my sister Mary and me in San Bruno near the National Archives, which houses Chinese immigration files.

We may never find the answer, but what we did discover was that Leland's grandfather, Loo Gan Heung, and my grandfather were cousins. We determined that Leland's father, Poy Wong (aka Paul Wong) and my father, Frank Jung, were second cousins. It was Leland's grandfather, born in 1880, who operated a laundry in Chattanooga around the early 1920s or earlier who helped bring my father come to the U. S. in 1921! A few years later, he helped his sons, Poy Wong and Hay Yee, with their immigration to Chattanooga, where each of them ran a laundry.

Now why was Leland so eager to find me? Well, he had retrieved his father's immigration file from the National Archives at San Bruno, California, a while back. He noticed that a Frank Wong, identified as the brother of his father, had testified on behalf of Leland's father when he was interrogated for admission to the United States. Leland did not know anything else about Frank Wong, and hoped that I might be able to help since I knew so much about the Chinese laundrymen in the South. At our meeting at my brother's house, which was not far from the National Archives in San Bruno that houses immigration files for thousands of Chinese immigrants, we examined his documents and discussed the possibility that this Frank Wong could have been a "paper," rather than a biological, brother.

Loo Gan Heung, the grandfather of Leland Wong.

I then recalled that about 40 years ago, my father came from San Francisco to visit me in Long Beach and asked me to drive him to meet a Chinese who worked at the legendary Far East Café in the Little Tokyo section of Los Angeles and to visit a Chinese named Frank Wong in Monterey Park. He might well have been the same man! I vaguely recall they were either distant relatives or men from my father's village in China.

From our conversation, I realized that I had known Leland's cousin, Jimmy Yee, back around 1960. His family had moved from Chattanooga to San Francisco in the early 1950s. I had lost contact with him and not known anything about him for the past 50+ years! Leland put me in touch with Yee who sent me a photograph of his grandfather, Loo Gan Heung, who as mentioned earlier, was the grand uncle who helped my father immigrate in 1921. Seeing a photograph for the first time of Loo Gan Heung was indeed an emotional moment that gave me a stronger connection to my father's history.

James Loo as a young man and several decades later.

Leland Wong told me about another Chinese laundryman, James Loo, who he had visited in his Charlotte, North Carolina, laundry in 1977. It appears he is a relative, but exactly how he is related to us is not clear. According to a family history compiled by Wing Loo, one of his sons, James Loo was born in 1899 in the village of Ha Mun Lay. At age 19, he came to the U. S. and worked in several cities in the South, first at a relative's laundry in Macon and then as a dishwasher in a Chinese restaurant in Birmingham, Alabama, before opening an unsuccessful laundry in Meridian, Mississippi. He moved to New York to work for a while before returning to work in a relative's laundry in Atlanta and then Chattanooga before settling in Charlotte to run a laundry in the 1940s.

I contacted Peggy Lore, another distant relative, although it is not clear exactly how she is related to me either. Her family had owned a laundry in Fayetteville, North Carolina, and she was now living in Colorado where she is an administrator at the University of Denver. She recalled visiting James Loo in Charlotte when she was growing up in Fayetteville, and believes that he is a relative, but she did not know the exact relationship either.

I guess the more you dig, the more you find! When I wrote *Southern Fried Rice*, I thought I had exhausted my sources on family history. There were several relatives who resolutely declined to share any information, so fearful that that any disclosures might have adverse consequences from immigration authorities. I did not think I would find any more family history information. Then, out of nowhere, this new information about James Loo, although somewhat vague, surfaced after all these years.

Fan mail requests

Writing is by necessity a solitary activity. Even after a book is published, the author rarely interacts directly with readers. Some, but not most, readers may post comments and numerical ratings on book websites that help the author see how readers feel about his or her work. At book signings, you meet a few people who have read your book and who might offer generous compliments, but most of the audience probably has yet to read your work. Once in a while I will receive a letter or an email in which a reader offers detailed comments and constructive suggestions in addition to varying degrees of praise. Several extraordinary emails from readers included more than comments, questions, or compliments on the contents of my books.

Stan Solamillo, who had researched the history of the earliest Chinese immigrants in Dallas, Texas, emailed to thank me for writing *Chinese Laundries*. He shared his article about Chinese laundrymen of the late 19th and early 20th century in Dallas.[7] In researching his article, he had compiled a detailed list of Dallas Chinese from 1873 to 1940 based on several public sources of data, information in tabular form that was not included with his article due to space considerations. We both felt that a list[8] of their actual names, addresses, and occupations of these pioneers could be useful for other researchers someday and I offered to post this data on my Chinese laundry website.[9]

One unusual email request came from a mother in Pennsylvania with an adopted daughter, about age 8, from China. After reading *Southern Fried Rice*, she needed an answer for a question raised by her daughter after she learned in school about racial segregation in the Jim Crow days of the Deep South from viewing a video about Martin Luther King Jr. She wondered, "If there were still Colored and White drinking fountains," which one would she, a Chinese, drink from?

My reply was that during the time when I was growing up in Macon, I never had any trouble using white public facilities, but I have learned that whether Chinese were treated as black or white varied from one town to another.

Another email came from a woman who had attended one of my book signings and purchased a copy of *Southern Fried Rice*. In her email, she related how meaningful my memoir was for her personally because when she was a child her family had made a move clear across the country that was the reverse of my family's move from Georgia to San Francisco. They went from the San Francisco Bay Area where there is a large Chinese community to northern Virginia where there were very few Chinese and the region was not very receptive to minorities. She shared her surprise when she read the section about my older sister getting married in San Francisco. Upon seeing my sister's married name, she suddenly realized that her mother and my sister had worked together a generation ago to develop Chinese cultural activities for children in their community. She thanked me for writing the book as it "made me feel a sense of connection which is lacking in my day-to-day existence and sense of identity. I've spent the better part of my life denying my Chinese heritage, trying to 'prove my American-ness.'"

A woman in Georgia contacted me by email, seeking help finding information about her African American husband's Chinese great grandfather. The KKK killed the father in the 1920s, and the family fled Georgia. She wanted to document the family history and was excited to find my book, which she felt was a valuable missing link. Sadly, I was not able to find any information for her.

About a week later, I found the following message on my Facebook page from an African American community college student in California asking for help in getting information related to her grandfather who had lived in the Mississippi Delta. She apparently was familiar with my book on the Delta Chinese, *Chopsticks in the Land of Cotton*, which is probably what led her to contact me.

> I'm a Japanese Major ... I have recently been researching the Chinese Mississippi Delta movement. My mother was born in Clarksdale, MS. My Aunt said that Her father spoke Chinese and I believe was also half Chinese due to his mother. He worked at one of the Chinese grocery stores that emerged at the time in Clarksdale. I believe my mom said it called Bing Li Way? I don't know much about my grandfather because he died when my mom was 10 in 1975. She said that the store was changed to a Piggly Wiggly. Does this store sound familiar? I really want to know more about this movement and about my grandfather's Chinese ancestry. I plan on buying your book too as well!!! This is so fascinating! Thank you so much! I hope to hear back from you!
>
> N__

Unaccustomed to receiving messages on Facebook, I did not discover her message *until over a year later*. As soon as I read it, I immediately tried to get back in touch with her.

> Hi N thanks for your msg, which unfortunately I never noticed...that is why I am so slooow in replying. I will ask some of my Delta contacts if 'Bing Li Way' rings a bell. And, yes, Piggly Wiggly (what a Southern name) was (is) a

grocery chain. I do see there was a Joe Bing Grocery in Clarksdale back around the 1960s on 6th St. You might be interested in a webpage I created for the Delta Chinese… http://mississippideltachinese.webs.com

best wishes,
John Jung

Sadly, I did *not* get a quick reply from N__ nor anytime soon. Checking her Facebook page, I could see that she did not use it much. I concluded she would probably never see my reply. Then, just before Thanksgiving 2012, about seven months after my reply to her, I received the following reply from N_.

Hi Mr. Jung.

I contacted (you) prior to the beginning of the year about a Chinese grocery store in Clarksdale, MS around the 60s & 70s that my grandfather had worked for. I did some more research through your website, and I found an oral interview with a Dan Bing, whose father was Joe Bing. It turns out that he did own Joe Bing Grocery, as well as a Bing Leeway store. When I read this in the interview, I cried because this is the same store that my mother had visited my grandfather! My grandfather, Jesse Lee Cooper, was a stocker at Bing Leeway. He himself, also owned a restaurant while working at Bing Leeway, called Fair Deal Cafe. My Aunt also remembers hearing my grandfather speaking Chinese in the store.
I would love to know more about the Bing's and what kind of people they were, as well as what other relations my grandfather had with them, if you know of any other information about them or how to contact them (Dan).
I appreciate your knowledge and research that is educating me about this time in history! It is important to me because the Bing's treated my grandfather so well!
Thank you so much for everything! Happy Thanksgiving!
N_

I was greatly relieved that N_ eventually checked her Facebook and found my reply and that she took my suggestion to access the website I created for the Mississippi Delta Chinese where I had included a link to the newly formed Mississippi Delta Chinese Heritage Museum on the campus of Delta State University. The museum has a collection of more than 20 recent interviews of Delta Chinese about the lives of Chinese grocery store families in the Delta.

As N- noted in her above reply to me, one of these interviews was with Dan Bing who mentioned the Clarksdale store of his father, Joe Bing, the very store where N's grandfather had worked as a stocker back in the '60s or '70s. I hope that N_ will be able to learn more about the past from Dan, but even if she does not, I believe she has gained a stronger connection with her family history. For me, it is gratifying to learn that my writing has been helpful to others in many ways that I did not anticipate. It is wonderful for an author to hear about such fascinating discoveries from readers. I hope more of them are in store in the future!

In 2014 I received an email from a professor in Pennsylvania who was excited because she had just learned about my book on Chinese laundries. She grew up in her family's laundry in Salisbury, North Carolina, and was curious to know if I had done any research on Chinese laundries in North Carolina.

> I was born and raised in Salisbury, N. C. and my family ran the only Chinese laundry there. My great Uncle ran a laundry in High Point, N. C. All of us in the surrounding area: Charlotte, Hickory, Greensboro, etc. formed a very tight network.

It was improbable but it so happened that I had actually noticed this Chinese laundry, the only one in Salisbury, several months earlier when I was examining census records to identify Chinese in the state of North Carolina. The reason I remembered it was because I had been trying to see if a specific laundry listed in one census, say, 1920, was still in business at the same site in a later census, say, 1930, and operated by the same person. Salisbury had only one Chinese laundry in 1920 and in 1930, but the addresses were different. I wondered whether there had been two different laundries or whether there had been just one laundry but it had been moved to a different address over the decade.

In a follow-up email, the professor mentioned, almost as an afterthought, that one of her university colleagues was a Chinese whose father had a laundry in Lambertville, New Jersey. What an improbable coincidence! Believe it or not, I had actually spoken a few weeks earlier by telephone with the owner, John Louie, of that laundry.

Why did I phone Louie in the first place? In the course of trying to locate Chinese laundries that were still operating, I had noticed a listing on the Web for the one Lambertville named "Sam Lee Laundry," which was one of the most frequent names for Chinese laundries. In fact, it was the name of my parents' laundry.

However, since few Chinese laundries still exist today, I wondered if Chinese ran this particular laundry or whether it might be a former Chinese laundry that retained its original name but was no longer run by Chinese. To satisfy this curiosity I called the laundry and learned from the owner, John Louie, that he was a fourth-generation Chinese owner.

When I disclosed this information to the professor, she shared it with her colleague, who she discovered was a brother of John Louie, the owner of Lambertville's long-standing Sam Lee Laundry!

Ask the right questions of the right people, and with a bit of luck, it is surprising what interesting stories you will uncover. Think how many other fascinating stories exist that we never discover because we didn't have the curiosity to look closely or the perceptiveness to detect interconnections.

Endnotes

[1] Krishan Saxena, an Indian American and colleague for many years, observed that similar family conflicts existed among some Indian immigrants as they struggled for economic success.

[2] http://chapelboro.com/?powerpress_pinw=36357-podcast

[3] http://tinyurl.com/qhg8x6j

[4] A few years ago, I visited historian, Mel Brown, in Austin, TX. His friend, Ron, was talking about blue grass music so I mentioned that a former student, Sharon Poss, had been in a blue grass band years ago when she was in graduate school at Duke but I lost track of her after she moved to Texas. Ron surprised me with the news that Sharon lived in Austin. He noted that her stint as a dee-jay on a local radio station would be over in an

hour and she would be headed to a local joint to jam with other fiddlers. We dashed over there to arrive before she did and had fun surprising her when she arrived.

At a book talk I gave in Long Beach, I had a wonderful surprise. JoRae Zuckerman, a stellar student from the very first class I taught at Long Beach State College in 1962 who I had not seen for half a century attended. I was delighted to learn that she had retired after a successful career as a psychology professor!

In 2013, a contact I had in Sacramento, Eileen Leung, suggested to Ed Soon that he should contact me for help in publicizing some old newspaper articles that described the civic contributions of his restaurateur father back in the late 1930s and early 1940s in Memphis. He had organized fund-raising events for China's struggle against Japan's invasion during World War II. I was pleased to help by blogging about his father's efforts. When Ed later learned that Rosie Chu had interviewed me in 2006 about *Southern Fried Rice* on her television program, he informed me that she was his cousin.

Brenda Jue Chinn, who I knew from our teen years in San Francisco but had not seen for over 50 years, was surprised to see a photograph of her uncle, Ray Joe, in my book about the Delta Chinese. She found my website and contacted me. Learning that Ray Joe was her uncle was fascinating because I knew from my Delta Chinese contacts that, like his brother in San Francisco, Ray Joe was a very influential person in the Delta Chinese community. Both brothers were made from the same cloth!

I knew two Chinese named Mel Lee from my teen years in San Francisco. One of them, now the operator of a large residential facility for Chinese elders, contacted me, out of the blue, to arrange to meet when I came to speak in San Francisco. A few days later when I spoke at Foster City, the *other* Mel Lee that I used to car pool with to school attended. So, within a few days, two Mel Lee's from my distant past and I were reconnected through my book talks.

I had not been in contact with Chinese students from Lowell High School in San Francisco since we graduated in 1955. But in 2012, Rosie Soo Hoo, a leader of the Lowell Chinese Student Club, hosted a get-together for some Chinese classmates. I found that one classmate, Richard Cheu, was also engaged in studying the lives of children of Chinese immigrants. He had collected oral histories that date back to the 1930s, and is working on a book about their lives. It is remarkable that Richard and I, from the same homeroom in high school, were now both actively engaged in writing about Chinese American history!

During my research for my book about the Mississippi Chinese, I had tried in vain to locate Robert Seto Quan, author of an excellent book published in 1982, *Lotus Among the Magnolias*. No one seemed to know what had happened to him and even Internet searches came up empty. Imagine my surprise when at a recent gathering of Chinese interested in family history, a woman told me that her ex-husband had written a book about the Mississippi Chinese. This was a surreal moment during which I learned that Quan had left the field of history after he published his book from his ex-wife.

[5] http://www.bbc.co.uk/radio4/factual/chinese_in_britain7.shtml

[6] https://www.facebook.com/groups/wguisfct/

[7] http://texashistory.unt.edu/ark:/67531/metapth35087/m1/18/

[8] http://chineselaundry.wordpress.com/2012/08/14/chinese-in-dallas-move-from-laundries-to-restaurants-1875-1940/

[9] http://chineselaundry.wordpress.com/

9 Promoting Books

Don't Hide Your Light Under A Bushel

No matter how interesting and well written your books are, how do you inform the potential audiences that they exist and where they can get them? Major book publishers invest in advertising and marketing for the books they publish, and hopefully recoup their expenses through profits on sales. Few self-published authors, however, can afford that method. However, the advantage that authors published by major publishers have may be exaggerated. For one matter, these publishers have many books to promote, and unless your book is a best-seller, after some initial promotion, they will ignore your book and turn their attention to promoting their newest books. In contrast, self-published authors can, and should, promote their books over a longer period. When you are a self-publisher, as I am, you have to devise your own means of publicity and promotion, without which it is unlikely that you will sell many copies. (And, you can't count on relatives and friends to buy many, especially since many of them expect complimentary copies.)

Promotion at book talks

Since my books are on Chinese American history, a topic for which the market is arguably not very large and one that is concentrated in regions with sizable Chinese populations, I soon realized that I had to find ways to hold book events such as talks and signings to generate awareness and interest. Although I anticipated some discomfort at having to "toot my own horn" with such activities, I soon overcame these concerns and even came to look forward to them. Once a professor, always a professor, eager to have an audience to lecture! My 40 years of teaching college students, some often inattentive, served me well in being at ease in giving book talks. The people at one venue enjoyed my talks enough to invite me four times, so I got to speak on each of my four books. I have given two or three talks at about five or six other sites. Counting events through October of 2014, I have surprised myself by making numerous public appearances across the country to speak about my books. These events have not only led to book sales but the opportunity to meet many interesting people as well as make contacts for other speaking events.

How did I manage to arrange all of these talks? Did I have a press agent or manager book these events? If I had an agent or publicist to find venues for me to give talks about my books, it would be wonderful.[1] My opportunities for speaking engagements have come from a mixture of luck (being in the right place at the right time), chutzpah and aggressive cold calls, and endorsements from contacts in a growing network that have connections with various organizations and groups interested in Chinese American history.

Social media promotion

Self-published authors must be resourceful. They first need to make efforts to identify and build networks of potential readers, a task made much easier than ever with the advent of popular free social media, such as Facebook[2] and Twitter,[3] where they can generate some "buzz'," or at least curiosity about their work, such as my Yin and Yang Press books. I post news and information about Chinese American history that I continue to discover since publishing my books on these social media.

All this self-promotion is work, but also fun, if you like playing with Internet resources. Initially, I was reluctant, even embarrassed, to engage in such aggressive marketing, but then I realized that if I didn't promote my books, they would not reach their intended audiences. As I gained experience, I found it easier to generate Web material, and the fact that so many people have told me that they found my books worthwhile reading helped me overcame any hesitation at engaging in sometimes shameless self-promotion!

Other free resources where independent authors can promote their work include goodreads.com.[4] On this website authors can generate awareness and interest in their work by offering free copies to readers who sign up for book drawings. I attracted several hundred readers expressing "interest" in the copies of my four books that I gave away but I do not know how that translated into sales. I also took advantage of free Web resources to promote my books by writing blogs and posting videos and interviews on sites like *YouTube* and *vimeo.com*. Reader reviews and personal recommendations can also be found on websites such as *Amazon.com,* which can affect sales of your books.

You don't need to promote your book to the whole world to succeed. It makes more sense to focus the campaign on groups that would have a strong interest in your topic. In the case of Chinese American history, there are Chinese community organizations, historical societies, and Chinese American history museums, for example, which have more interest in this topic than the general public would.

My *About.me* digital "business card."

To receive invitations to speak and to attract people to come hear you, it is essential that you establish who you are and why someone interested in the topic should believe that you have the credentials or authority to write or speak about it. I used a website, *About.me*,[5] that enabled me to create a profile of "who I am" by describing my background and experience. In other words, you need some degree of credibility to attract the identified audiences. Because I had a long career as university professor, even though it was in psychology and not history, that background and experience were still invaluable for writing books since I had published several textbooks in psychology.

Book promotion on websites

List of my talk venues on weebly.com with a photograph of cousins Dominic, William, Cynthia (Dominic's wife), Veronica, and Henry at 2010 Atlanta talk.

I used the Web to advantage by creating a "book tour'" to publicize my book events on weebly.com,[6] one of the many excellent resources for free website creation. On it I listed the places and dates where I spoke, and included photographs of the events, compliments from readers and audience members around the country and links to videos of some of my presentations. Sometimes I embedded the videos on my sites to increase the chances that readers will view them. Some of the videos are hosted on *YouTube*. By cross-linking these various sites, I can increase the traffic to all of them and hopefully create more awareness and interest in my books. As I gained experience in creating websites, I reformatted the book tour information and included other information about my books on a second website.[7] Creating a list of the more than 80 book talks and signings as of late-2014 on my four books, as shown in the Appendix, provides a valuable "track record" that is useful in getting other invitations to give book talks.

wix.com catalog for Yin and Yang Press.

Online sales have become a dominant factor for the book publishing industry. Brick-and-mortar bookstores may soon go the way of dinosaurs. Many people who want to buy a book go to the gorilla of online book sales, Amazon, where any book with an ISBN number is listed, often with an option to *LOOK INSIDE* for a sample of the book, and comments from some readers. Amazon allows authors to promote their books by posting photos, a video, and feeds from a blog on their own Author Page.[8] I also created Author Pages for my books on other websites such as Lulu.com,[9] and Createspace.com.[10]

In addition, self-published authors can create more extensive promotion of their work through an increasing number of free or inexpensive tools on the Internet that can be periodically updated and expanded. For example, I created one free website[11] on wix.com that serves as a "catalog" for Yin & Yang Press to showcase my four books. I provide not only descriptive summaries of each book but also excerpts and comments from readers, audiences at book talks, and scholars. I also include photographs of audiences and book buyers to illustrate the interest that the books generated.

I also placed free widgets on my websites from Freado.com[12] and bookdaily.com[13] that let me make sample pages from each book available for browsing.

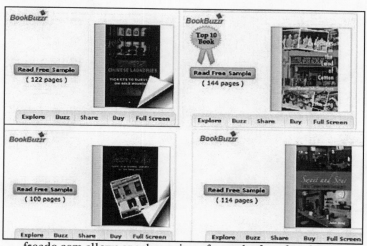

freado.com allows sneak previews for each of my four books.

Of course, while you save time and gas money by not having to go to a store, you have to pay shipping costs for online book purchases. Enter the e-book, which has its pros and cons, but may be here to stay. Although the price of e-book is much lower than paper books, and the profit is also reduced, volume of sales may increase because buyers may feel the e-versions, such as for the Kindle e-reader, are more affordable. Book publishing is rapidly changing, and authors need to keep up to date with the newer technology. Thus, to reach a larger audience for each of my books I created kindle versions.[14]

Authors must work hard to promote and market their books that they spent so much time and effort in researching and writing. Most self-publishers cannot afford advertising and other expensive book promotions, but the Web offers many free resources that authors can use to generate some publicity about their books. For example, I created a separate website for each of my four books.[15] On each book site, I included a blog that I can update periodically to provide additional material related to the theme of each book so that interested readers will have reason to revisit each site.

Chineselaundry.wordpress.com

My site on Chinese laundries[16] includes photographs of many early laundries, excerpts from newspaper articles dating back to the late 1800s that refer to Chinese laundrymen and other information of historical interest on the topic.

I created *Yin & Yang ex/Press/ions*, digital magazines using glossi.com, for each of my four books, with links between them as

166

well as to other issues of the magazines with material that supplemented a book. For example, Issue 7 of *Yin & Yang ex/Press/ions*[17] included links to presentations described in Chapter 5 made by Flo Oy Wong, Nellie Wong, Bill Tong, and Julie Hornsby Wong at some of my book talks about their own family restaurant experiences described in *Sweet and Sour*.

Yin & Yang ex/Press/ions digital magazine Issue No. 7.

Promotion via Chinese media

When I gave a talk in 2012 at the Torrance, California Library, *China News*, a mainland China media organization sent a reporter and film crew to film parts of the talk and interview me afterwards.

China News coverage, Torrance Library talk, *Chopsticks in the Land of Cotton.*

In May 2013, Emma Wong, a writer for *World Journal,* a Chinese newspaper in the U. S., requested an interview about my background and the content of my books, which was published (in Chinese) to reach Chinese with no or limited English language facility.

World Journal publicity for Yin and Yang Press books.

One might think there would be a good market for my books in China, Hong Kong, and Taiwan, especially in areas from which most Chinese who came to North America originated. However, I would need to have my books translated into Chinese and find some means for distribution in China. However, the logistics involved are daunting and even though I have had some limited queries, nothing has yet materialized.

A promising development in 2014 was the discovery and interest in my books by a writer in Beijing, Shuhua Dai. She interviewed me and wrote an article about my books for *China Narratives,*[18] an e-zine published in Chinese aimed at the Chinese market. Hopefully, it will stimulate interest in my work in China!

From article about my books in *China Narratives,* July 2014 by Shuhua Dai.

Promotion by book donations

Some people assume Yin and Yang Press is a flourishing publishing company and send requests for donations of books for worthy causes. So far, I have donated copies of *Southern Fried Rice* to a fund-raising raffle for a school for girls in Hawaii, other titles to two Chinese historical societies, a set of all four titles to the Overseas Chinese Museum in Guangdong, China, and a set for raffle prizes at the annual celebration of Chinese New Year by the Asian Pacific Islanders Network at California State University, Long

Beach. The past two years I have donated sets to my alma mater, the University of California, Berkeley, for a fund-raising auction.

Donation of book sets to the University of California Christmas auction.

And, one year I fulfilled a request to donate copies of *Sweet and Sour* as raffle prizes at performances of a comedy nightclub show, *Kosher Kung Pao Christmas*, in San Francisco!

Flier for Kung Pao Kosher Comedy show.

It is gratifying that these contributions of my books can help these organizations. I honor these requests for altruistic reasons, but also because they create publicity for Yin and Yang Press books.

Endnotes

[1] In 2013 a literary agent noticed *Southern Fried Rice* and convinced me to have her submit it to a publisher. On one hand, I thought the book was doing well without an agent, but then I thought, why not? Unfortunately, despite her diligent efforts we have not yet found a publisher. Fortunately, the memoir has sold well as a self-published book.

[2] https://www.facebook.com/YinandYangPress

[3] https://twitter.com/jrjung

[4] http://www.goodreads.com/author/list/231019.John_Jung

[5] http://about.me/yinandyangpress

[6] http://yinandyangpress.weebly.com/

[7] http://yinandyangpress.webs.com/

[8] http://www.amazon.com/John-Jung/e/B001IXO5CW

[9] http://www.lulu.com/shop/search.ep?type=&keyWords=john+jung&x=0&y=0&sitesearch=lulu.com&q=

[10] http://tinyurl.com/lrqvcja

[11] http://wix.com/yinandyang/yinandyangpress

[12] http://www.freado.com/users/books/26435/john-jung

[13] http://www.bookdaily.com/author/1105419/john-jung

[14] http://www.amazon.com/John-Jung/e/B001IXO5CW/ref=dp_byline_cont_book_1

[15] Southern Fried Rice: Life in A Chinese Laundry in the Deep South

   Chinese Laundries: Tickets to Survival on Gold Mountain

   Chopsticks in the Land of Cotton: Lives of Mississippi Delta Chinese Grocers

   Sweet and Sour: Life in Chinese Family Restaurants

[16] http://chineselaundry.wordpress.com/

[17] http://glossi.com/yinyang/85520-stories-from-chinese-family-restaurants

[18] http://slides.com/jrjung/introducing-yin-yang-press-books-in-china#/

10 Kudos

As previously mentioned, authors do not get to meet most of their readers in person. And, even at book readings and signings, audience members do not all share their reactions with authors. Consequently, when authors receive comments from readers about how they felt about a book, whether in person or from letters and emails, it is valuable feedback, even if the reactions are not always positive.

Praise from readers

Readers want to contact authors for many different reasons. Some of my readers wrote to thank me because they felt that reading about the early history of Chinese in North America helped them visualize and appreciate the experiences of their immigrant parents or grandparents. Here are some comments I received from different readers:

Southern Fried Rice gave me a window into what life might have been like for my own family even though my relative most likely arrived in the 1870s.

I devoured your book with great interest! I was reading with fingers crossed that perhaps a resource might pop up that might aid me in finding additional documentation of my ancestor(s). There is a vague story of my great-grandmother being Chinese or half Chinese. As a child she and her mother worked as seamstresses for a private family. Her mother making clothes for the daughter while she made matching clothes for the doll. I'm told that my great-grandmother died from headaches that they believed came from her having been hit or beaten by those she worked for. The details of the story shifts depending on who's telling it, but this is the story more or less. There is no question there is Chinese ancestry amongst our varied heritage of African, Native American and European bloodlines as the physical features are imprinted on our faces.

I thoroughly enjoyed this book! I learned much that will hopefully give me some leads in searching for information on my paternal grandfather... even if I never find anything, your book has allowed me to gain some insight into what his life might have been life, what he might have experienced as the only Chinese in St. Augustine, FL, and how he came to be there.

I appreciated that you wrote this book (Chinese Laundries), because it has given me a deeper perspective in what it means to be a second generation Chinese American of emigrant parents who operated a Chinese laundry. I understand that all minorities that immigrated to the United States in search of a better life had their struggles with survival and discrimination, this makes me not only value and respect my parents, but for other emigrant parents who desired their children to be prosperous.

After reading personal and brilliantly written accounts of the blood, sweat, and toil that Chinese Americans endured in the development of the laundry empire in America, you will never feel the same way about the mundane chore of loading and unloading your washer/dryer again. This book doesn't just take you through the historical trajectory of the occupation oft-times associated with Chinese immigrants; it's the story of a people - of families who believe in the value of hard work and determination, and the undying hope of a brighter future. This book is an absolute must-read for anyone of Chinese descent; more importantly, it is for anyone who has a dream.

Other readers wrote to express a personal connection with the author's experiences or observations that helped them with their understanding of their own cultural experiences and recognition of their ethnic identity. I was surprised that many other Chinese, even those living in Chinese communities felt they were not "Chinese enough" as I had felt from not growing up with Chinese American peers.

... I read with real enthusiasm about your personal experiences living in the South and about your motivation to write a book about your parents. I think I can relate to some of what you went through, being from an immigrant family, and going through the settlement process.

Looking back, I had great experiences with prejudice but didn't know it at the time. I did not turn to my parents (mother spoke poor English, father was always too busy in grad school) so basically I stood up for myself. I was constantly "assaulted" by white kids, verbal taunts, name-calling, pebble throwing, etc. Teachers turned a blind eye to all these events. I knew something was wrong but had no clue if I had any recourse except to stand up for myself, which I did.

There were a total of 3 minorities in my elem. school. Myself, 1 black girl, Yolanda, and 1 Korean boy who just arrived from Korea, spoke no English, didn't even know the kids were picking on him. Yolanda and I spent our time together far in the back of the "yard" under the pecan tree, away from the white kids who constantly picked on us. I think the only thing that "saved" me was I was a very successful student. Well, we're all grown up now, and thank goodness things are much better for our children, even in the South and us.

After reading the chapter on "Lives of Chinese Laundry Children" I felt great pride in my unique experiences (growing up in a laundry), and was very happy to have my thoughts and feelings normalized.

I grew up knowing only the few Chinese laundries in the Washington DC area, and some of our cousins in New York. But I never thought much about the common threads until I started looking through your books. Thanks for the education and the enlightenment!

...I completely understood your sense of feeling "not being Chinese enough" (from being the only Chinese in town). Even today, when I am in a room full of Chinese adults, I feel like a foreigner, with too much "white" attitude to be Chinese. I think that it was my growing up, isolated from other CHINESE that caused me to have "confusion" and identity crisis of sorts. Not only was I the ONLY Chinese kid in Baton Rouge, La., I was also an only child, in a typical Chinese family (be seen but not heard), so I led a very lonely existence. I did not make a Chinese friend until I was in the 4th grade, when we moved back to New Orleans. Up until then I had very little exposure to any other Chinese family. My mother did her best to keep the "Chinese" in me, forcing me to speak Mandarin and teaching me to write basic Chinese words, both of which I still can do. (I am grateful now of course for her strict, strident rules!)

Some readers wrote to testify about the accuracy of my portrayal of the life and experiences for Chinese in an earlier time and express how valuable these books will be for the younger generation. Some even told me they purchased my books for their grandchildren.

I am a friend of most of the people you interviewed in your book (Chopsticks in the Land of Cotton). I recently finished reading your book and felt I was right among the people you interviewed. It's the best book written about the Chinese in the Mississippi Delta.

You've made some amazing observations, wrote them down with sincerity, and I wholeheartedly support you on it. You've brought back some fond memories and I'm sure it will touch other folks like myself that have gone through it.

...your book presents the most definitive and accurate account of the Chinese in the Ms Delta - what it was like to be Chinese and growing up in the segregated South during that time. Thanks for all your time and effort in researching and telling the story of the Ms Chinese Grocers in the Land of Cotton.

As a first generation Chinese growing up in my parents' restaurant, I want to say thank you for your great book: Sweet and Sour.

"Thank you for writing this book especially so that current and future young people with roots in the South will know about their roots..."

I have read both books by John Jung about Chinese laundries. The first was about his growing up in a Chinese laundry in Macon, GA, my hometown. I was several years younger than John, and did not know him. What a fascinating story about being the only Chinese family in a town of 80,000 people and the struggles and discrimination the family went through. The second book is a thoroughly researched book about Chinese laundries in the U. S. and Canada as well as about early Chinese restaurants. If you want to know about how emigrants to this country who spoke little or no Chinese fared, this is the book for you. If you are Chinese, it should make you very proud of your heritage.

Praise from audiences

The content of my books and my presentations about them at book signings obviously have much in common, but the tasks of writing and speaking are quite different. One can write a good book, but not deliver a good spoken presentation, or vice versa. When I began doing book talks, my years of college classroom teaching were of great benefit. I had no speaker anxiety, spoke clearly, and knew how to organize my material. Still, effective communication with an audience consisting generally of much older members of the community and a classroom of college students is not the same. College courses are more formal, while public talks can be more relaxed and include more anecdotes and humor. I quickly adjusted to the differences, however, and soon felt very comfortable and effective in establishing rapport with my audiences, as the following comments from many audiences across the country show.

You were a hoot! Thanks for coming to speak at Sacramento Chinese Culture Foundation... the greatest testimonial is no one left after dinner! The audience was mesmerized by your style and candor. Even the Chinese-born audience said they learned something new.

It was a pleasure meeting you today @ Delta State U & well worth the 2-hr drive. I am look'g forward to read' your books and will share them among our 3 college-age daughters. Your time and patience in document'g grow'g up in America in the early years will help visualize to the younger generation what our ancestors went through.

We were honored to have you visit (Chinese American Museum of Chicago). Everyone really enjoyed your presentation and company-one of the best comments was _ he was so down to earth and engaging.

The Berkeley Chinese Community Church Senior Center has been twice blessed with your presentations, last year on "Chinese Laundries" and this year on "Southern Fried Rice." You have a way of telling your stories that bring back so many memories of our own lives as we all grew up as 2nd generation Chinese Americans. We look forward to a presentation on your 3rd book "Chopsticks in the Land of Cotton" with great anticipation.

I am grateful for your willingness to share your story with us last Saturday in Washington, D. C. I felt like you overwhelmed the audience and left them wanting to hear more...We have heard nothing but positive comments from many of the folks who attended.

Each time John Jung comes to the (San Diego Historical) museum to present his books about the experience of Chinese laundries, Chinese markets, being the only Chinese family in town, and now, Sweet and Sour: Life in Chinese Family Restaurants, so many Chinese immigrants and their children share in the experiences that he describes that it evokes the nostalgic atmosphere of a family reunion.

Wonderful talk on my favorite of all of your books! Thank YOU for being the object of our overwhelming attendance and I hope you sold a few books to the attendees! ... you proved that you were the "man of the hour!" Thank you for "being" our event.

Thanks for a great presentation!!!! As I told you earlier today, my friends were greatly impressed with you and your info on Chinese families of restaurant owners... it is an honor to meet you and hope to see more of you again in Portland.

We, the younger generation of Chinese Americans, all appreciated your presentation of Sweet & Sour. The story is full of laughter and tears for the audiences.

What an informative and enjoyable talk on the history of Chinese laundries in America, and what an honor it is to meet author John Jung. I recommend everyone try to catch any of John Jung's talks!

These endorsements and expressions of the benefits experienced by audience members have been powerful rewards that more than compensate me for the time, effort, expense, and often fatiguing or frustrating experiences, involved in preparing and traveling to give talks about my books.

Praise from scholars

The positive reader and audience responses were, of course, very rewarding and gave me a sense of achievement of some important goals. My primary goal was to generate interest in Chinese American history among people in the community.

However, it was also important to me as someone who had a long career as a scholar, although in psychology, that my books pass muster with scholars in the field of Asian American studies and history. Not having been formally trained in the disciplines in which I was writing, I hoped I would receive a passing grade. Fortunately, my four books received positive reactions from many leading scholars!

Southern Fried Rice

...an incisive clarity that shines extra light on the mundane oddities and inhuman logic of everyday life in the South before the Civil Rights era...a rare glimpse at the fairly common experience of those Americans who found themselves in the impossible spaces of the American racial order, a world that is both thankfully distant and yet hauntingly familiar still. Henry Yu, Professor of History, University of British Columbia

...This engaging, candid, and often humorous and heartwarming book is an important contribution not only to the fields of psychology, sociology, and history but also to literature. Social scientists and students alike will find the book immensely fascinating and satisfying. Stanley Sue, Distinguished Professor of Psychology, University of California, Davis

Rich with historical details of immigration, John Jung's engaging memoir about growing up Chinese in the segregated South is an insightful observation about the resilience of Asian American families and the fluidity of culture and ethnic identities across different historical moments and racialized spaces. Barbara Kim, Asian American Studies, California State University, Long Beach

... insightful account of Chinese-American family life in the context of restraints on immigration and the U. S. racial and economic systems...offers valuable insight about economic struggles in difficult times, intergenerational relations, continuing ties to Chinese culture and community, family obligation, gender, the key role of laundries in Chinese economic opportunity, and much else...a charming and informative book. Paul Rosenblatt, Professor of Family Social Science, University of Minnesota

...a valuable mirror that will help move the history of those who are neither Black nor White towards a more deserving central role in the national and international human story. Stephanie Evans, Professor and Chair, African American Studies, Africana Women's Studies, and History Clark Atlanta University

This inside view of an immigrant family who struggled to make a living and to maintain connections with their Chinese heritage and homeland highlights the mutability and complexity of Chinese American identity and the frequently forgotten ethnic and racial diversity of the South. Krystyn Moon, Assistant Professor of History, Georgia State University

This interesting memoir presents a unique view of ethnic identity development. It provides fascinating insights into the process of learning what it means to be Chinese when there is no Chinese community, or even other Chinese families, to interact with, and the way subsequent experiences in - and out - of a Chinese community further shape this process. Jean Phinney, Professor of Psychology, California State University, Los Angeles, Multi-Group Ethnic Identity Measure Creator

...offers an intriguing and unique perspective on American immigration...highlights many features of the larger society, including both government policy and situational practice that affect the lives of immigrants, both then and now. Kay Deaux, Distinguished Professor of Psychology, City University of New York Graduate Center

A charming and engrossing self-ethnography...enhances the archive of Asians in the South as well as our understanding of how Jim Crow situated the Chinese between "white" and "colored." Leslie Bow, Professor of English & Asian American Studies, University of Wisconsin

Chinese Laundries

... comprehensive historical study of the Chinese laundries in the United States, a profound analysis of the psychological experiences of the Chinese laundrymen in America and their families in China; and above all, written by someone who has intimate experiences with the Chinese laundry, it is a tribute to those Chinese immigrants whose labor and sacrifice laid the foundation of the Chinese American community, and a testimony of the Chinese laundrymen's resilience, resourcefulness, and humanity. Renqiu Yu, Professor of History, State University of New York.

An academically solid effort that is much enhanced by several personal narratives from other "Children of the Laundries." This rewarding study ... is a long overdue analysis of a familiar experience hidden in plain sight. Mel Brown, *Chinese Heart of Texas, The San Antonio Chinese Community, 1875-1975.*

...a significant contribution to the history of Chinese laundries...best told by someone like Jung who experienced a 'laundry life,' and understands its psychological impact on the Chinese laundrymen and their families. . .Murray K. Lee, San Diego Chinese Historical Museum

What is remarkable is the combination of this historical perspective with Professor Jung's social psychological descriptions and analyses of laundrymen and their descendants. Their personal life stories, with inner thoughts, feelings, values, attitudes, work experiences and survival hardships are skillfully presented with penetrating insights and observations. This broad perspective presents an overall picture...
 Ban Seng Hoe, End*uring Hardship: The Chinese Laundry in Canada*

Chopsticks in the Land of Cotton

...As a Chinese American who grew up in the Deep South himself, John Jung has a degree of empathy that imbues Chopsticks in the Land of Cotton with an insight both in depth and breadth that is totally requisite for a study of this nature. Mel Brown, *Chinese Heart of Texas, The San Antonio Community, 1875-1975.*

John Jung has done it again! Plunging into the history of Chinese grocers in the Mississippi-Yazoo Delta, he traces their migration history, work, families, and social lives. His work is anchored in a creative mix of oral history, community historical documents and public records, and includes a generous fill of photos. As a study of the complexities of triangular race relations in the Jim Crow South, his work rivals James Loewen's classic study, *The Mississippi Chinese.*
 Greg Robinson, Professor of History, University of Quebec

Sweet and Sour: Life in Chinese Family Restaurants

"Sweet and Sour" covers many important aspects of the Chinese restaurant business and it is a great contribution to the study of Chinese food in America. This area really deserves more attention than it has had.
 Haiming Liu, Ethnic and Women's Studies, Cal Polytechic University

...This well-researched, thoughtfully conceptualized monograph brings academic rigor and adds historical depth, as well as the perspectives of an insightful scholar and a second-generation Chinese American, to our understanding of the development of Chinese food in the realm of public consumption in the United States and Canada. It promises to elevate that

understanding to a higher level... Through this book, I hope, consumers at the ubiquitous Chinese restaurants can also gain a deeper appreciation of historical forces and human experiences that have shaped the food they now enjoy.
Yong Chen, Professor of History, University of California, Irvine

John Jung has taken us down another memory lane and this time we brought along our appetite. "Sweet & Sour" evoked hundreds of memories of Chinatowns, favorite soul food dishes, haunts of opulent and garish banquet halls and the more frequented and beloved hole-in-the walls. These are the collective memories shared by families and friends. Sweet & Sour is also an anthropological study...Without a doubt this is by far Jung's best work and with the greatest universal appeal.
Sylvia Sun Minnick, S*AMFOW: The San Joaquin Chinese Legacy*

I greatly admired and enjoyed "Sweet and Sour" ...It does an excellent job of going over the historical background on early U. S. Chinese restaurants, unearthing lots of material new to me...interviews of Chinese restaurateurs opened up a whole new side to the story, of what it was like to work and live in these restaurants. Andrew Coe, *Chop Suey: A Cultural History of Chinese Food in the United States*

I am reading your delightful book, Sweet and Sour. I especially like the "Insider Perspectives" section. Those first-hand experiences can generate a lot of potentially testable hypotheses about how the Chinese were able to provision their remote restaurants with exotic ingredients while other ethnic groups could not. Susan B. Carter, *University of California, Riverside*

I was struck by how it is both a work of scholarship and a documentation of the experience of Chinese restaurant workers. It serves to teach us about their experiences on multiple levels. Heather Lee, Brown University

Praise from three bloggers

Some wonderful feedback from audience members came from bloggers who generously posted their positive reactions online. Jay Roberts, who attended my 2012 talk in Washington, posted this nice compliment about my presentation:

... In front of an audience of about 50, he spoke on the topic – "The Value of Learning and Teaching the History of Chinese in America That School Books Left Out."

…The author, who still retains a bit of a Southern accent, touched on a handful of themes. Isolation is a common one for immigrants, his own made worse by the fact they were the only Chinese people living in Macon (Georgia) between 1928 and 1956.

…Jung spoke not as a bitter man, and in fact revealed a sense of humor on several occasions. Nevertheless, he drew on a reservoir of stories that pointed out injustices, cruelty, and ignorance directed at him and his family.

After attending my 2012 talk in Portland, Oregon, Patrick McGraw made a post on his blog, PFMReports.com:

" ... It may look like it should have been dull. Add that it was a history lecture and you might be certain that it was dull. The lecturer was Dr. John Jung, who was born in Macon, Georgia, where he and his family were the only Chinese in town. Dr. John Jung spoke about the history of Chinese immigrants, but he told it through the stories of Chinese restaurants and the families that operate them. He managed to work the Chinese Exclusion Act and chop suey into one sentence! … As I have said before, history is not about dates, it's about stories. If more people could have a teacher like Dr. Jung, maybe fewer people would run from history…"

A third blogger, Christoph Fischer, read *Chinese Laundries* and published a favorable review accompanied by an interview with me about what led me to write the book and how I researched the content.[1]

I found *"Chinese Laundries: Tickets to Survival on Gold Mountain"* by John Jung on *Indietribe*, an independent writer's website and was intrigued by the title that suggested a subject way off the beaten track. I was not prepared for the ease with which I was able to read this academic study of Chinese Laundries in the US. 1/4 of the book is a bibliography, bearing witness to the vast amount of knowledge the author possesses and how much research he has done to give credibility to his account.

From casual to concrete discrimination, indirect legal victimization and tax laws to statistic, tables and photographs – a huge amount of details is given and documented.

Individual accounts of the workers and owners of laundries lend a great personal touch to the hardship, tragedies and persistence that these people endured.

Despite the often-sad stories and the description of inhumane and intolerant treatment this book is by no account a tale of self-pity and pointing the finger. The facts are described objectively and it accentuated the survival spirit of these people rather than their role as victims. After all, they are survivors.

With Tom Chan and my wife, Phyllis. Sacramento, CA. 2009.

Tom Chan, who took many splendid photographs at my talk in Sacramento in 2009, surprised me with a flattering email that began as follows:

> John...You're all over the Internet & up to the minute. I like your Gangnam Style of writing Chinese American History so it's not dull. Yeah, add some PSY zing to it.
> TOM... 93-year old guy

Not everyone has the time or inclination to express his or her reactions to a book or a talk by an author. So, it is always a pleasant surprise when people who have read one of my books or attended one of my talks take the time to share their reactions to the books.

Endnotes

[1] http://writerchristophfischer.wordpress.com/2013/02/24/chinese-laundries-tickets-to-survival-on-gold-mountain-by-john-jung/

11 Important Lessons Learned

勞思源

Your Chinese name is part of a famous Chinese proverb.

Growing up in Georgia I never had the opportunity or the interest in learning how to write or read Chinese. When we moved to San Francisco, my mother promptly enrolled me in a beginning Chinese language class at a nearby Chinese church. However, inasmuch as I was 15 years old, and all my classmates were about 6 or 7, and much faster learners than I, it was only a matter of days before I became a Chinese school dropout!

At some of my book tour sites, I am asked what my name is in Chinese. Although I can speak some limited toishan-wa, the only thing I can write in Chinese is my name because my parents taught me how to at any early age. Since I have rarely been asked to write it since childhood I lack confidence in my ability to write the Chinese characters correctly on the spur of the moment. My solution is to always carry a printed copy of my Chinese name.

When I gave a copy of my name written in Chinese to someone after a talk to the Sacramento Chinese Cultural Foundation, I was informed that my name was very interesting in that it was part of a famous Chinese proverb. This revelation startled me and I was eager to know exactly what my name meant. I learned that my given name included Chinese characters that were part of this proverb, *"When you drink water, remember the source."*

This discovery might make some think that my new career in tracking and celebrating the lives of the pioneer Chinese immigrants was, in effect, an unconscious attempt to live up to my Chinese name. It was as if a fortune cookie held the explanation of why I was so devoted to unearthing and sharing important findings about Chinese American history.

I realize that some people believe that a person's name is a prophecy. Alternatively perhaps people try to live up to the meaning of their name. Or the way some people treat a person might be affected by the meaning of their name. In my case, I did not know that my Chinese name had any symbolic meaning so I could not have been consciously trying to live up to my name by studying the roots of my family history. Yet, there is no mistaking that my four books on Chinese American history were at least coincidental evidence that my research reflected the meaning of the proverb associated with my Chinese name.

Audience questions

I have been fortunate to have many generous positive comments from audience members at the many talks I have made about my books across the country over the past seven or eight years.

I can generally predict what questions will come up after a book talk. Whenever I speak about *Southern Fried Rice*, my memoir about how our family lived as the only Chinese in Macon, Georgia back in the 1930s to 1950s, invariably someone will ask how or why we were in Georgia. Or, they want to know whether I attended a "White" or a "Colored" school or where I sat when riding a bus.

In the 1940s when I was a child, I never had any problems attending a white school in Macon. As for the question of whether I would be allowed to sit in the white section on a bus, I do not know. I never rode on a bus until 1950 because we lived in the business district and I could easily walk to any place I wanted to go. When I was 12 and entered junior high school, I had to ride the bus but I could sit anywhere.

At a talk I gave at the Torrance, California, library on my book, *Chopsticks in the Land of Cotton* about the history of Chinese in the Mississippi Delta, several questions dealt with race relations, mostly between Chinese and whites, but also one person asked about Chinese-black interactions. Such questions are not surprising since many West Coast audience members had never been to the South but were well-aware of the strong racial prejudices and segregation that existed there for many decades.[1]

I also got a few unexpected questions. Were the Chinese actively involved during the civil rights activism? Did Chinese kids enjoy blues music? How did blacks and Chinese get along socially? Did Chinese kids engage in the practice of martial arts?

These were challenging questions and I did not have definitive answers to some of them because my book focused on the history of Chinese in the Delta prior to the civil rights activism of the 1960s. Fortunately, I had several Chinese in my audience who grew up in Mississippi who were eager to answer these questions. Clearly, there is more work to be done and a need to examine more recent history to see how race relations changed since the 1960s!

I do also get questions that are challenging in more amusing ways such as, "What is your next book?" I used to say I have no plans for a future book, but after I "accidentally" came to write *Chopsticks in the Land of Cotton* and *Sweet and Sour,* I've learned to be less certain with my answer.

A related question is how long it takes me to write one of my books, which is sometimes asked by people who are dreaming of writing their own book and want to gauge how much effort is involved. Some will confide that they want to write a book and already have collected lots of material, but confess they have yet to write a single page. They want my advice on how to start. I understand their lack of confidence, which I experienced when I started my first book. I urge them to just start writing, one page at a time, because "Rome was not built in a day." I also urge them to ask others to read drafts so they can get feedback. I suggest that they consult the many excellent <u>free resources on websites</u>[2] that deal with many aspects of writing, self-publishing, and marketing books.

Another popular question is, "Which of your four books is your favorite?" I deflect the question by pointing out that it is similar to asking a parent, "Which of your children is your favorite?"

But I also have had rather odd questions as well, questions which called for calm and polite replies. In the first case, a woman in Macon prefaced her question with the compliment that I knew a lot. She then asked me how, in view of my knowledge, would I propose to solve some of the major problems in the world today. It was immediately clear that she was not trying to heckle me so I did not take offense. At the same, I felt I owed her some reply that would not be a put-down rather than to ignore her and proceed to another question. I simply noted that her question was important but that it was beyond my "expertise." After the talk, another member of the audience came to offer apologies for this woman who had a reputation of asking off-the-wall questions.

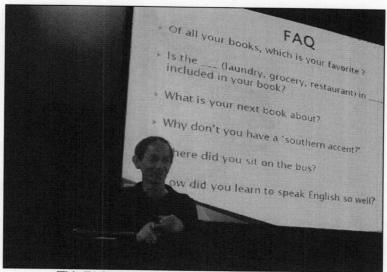

This FAQ slide is a fun ending I use for some talks.

Another challenging situation occurred during the Q&A following a talk in Foster City, California, about *Southern Fried Rice*, when a woman asked where my parents were naturalized. After I responded that my father was naturalized in Macon, Georgia, and my mother in San Francisco, she accused me of lying. I was taken aback, to say the least, and asked her why she felt I was not telling the truth. She claimed that she knew my parents were naturalized in Alabama, which I knew was not true. I simply told her again that she was mistaken, but she was not satisfied. I saw no point in continuing the fruitless argument, and moved on by calling on someone else.

After the session as I was gathering my unsold books, I noticed a CD on the corner of the table that was not mine despite the fact that it bore the name, "Jung," written in black with a

Sharpie pen. Apparently, my challenger had surreptitiously left it on the table for me. When I got access to a computer later, I let my curiosity get the better of me (for all I knew, the disk contained a virus). The CD contained a page from the 1930 U. S. census for Alabama and listed a Chinese couple with the surname Jung. My adversary had mistakenly jumped to the conclusion that these Jungs were my parents.

What still puzzled me was why she was so determined to show me up. She obviously had looked up this information in advance since she had burned it onto a CD. It was a strange encounter; the librarian later told me that this woman had engaged in other confrontations with other speakers in the past. I guess her mission in life was to try to embarrass or challenge speakers!

Ups and downs of book signings

Many people think of book signings as glamorous and happy occasions for authors. They can definitely be rewarding experiences, but one should realize there are also downsides. Arranging book talks is not always easy. I have encountered some frustration and aggravation many times!

A small independent author/publisher has to make many decisions in preparation. First, which audiences to seek to speak to? If you can arrange a talk to an audience that already has a strong interest in your topic, you are already well on the way to success. On the other hand, if you seek, or get invited by, a group that has little knowledge or interest in your topic, you will be "going uphill." In any case, you still need to be personable and create rapport with your audience to get and hold their attention. The way you present your talk should be tailored to fit the characteristics such as age, education level, and social class of your audience. Your experience and skill as a speaker can make or break your connection with an audience.

There are practical matters to consider as well. How many books should the author bring to the event? If you bring too many, there is the hassle and cost of taking them home. If you bring too few, you disappoint some people and lose some sales. The latter has so far not happened because being an optimist I have always brought too many books. If the event is local, I can easily put the unsold books in my car and take them home. But, as has been the case on several occasions in places like Atlanta, Chicago, Houston, and San Francisco, I found myself with more unsold books than I could readily carry back on the plane (especially with the airline charges for baggage). I have been very lucky in all of these cases to have local friends store the surplus books until the next time I came there to speak.

If I had a marketing manager, I wouldn't have to worry about arranging to deliver copies of my books to various venues. But since I do not, I have to do that task, like many other chores associated with book talks, myself. Many things can go wrong. One entire box of books I shipped to Mississippi "went missing" (I find this term a rather bizarre one, as if the books had minds of their own). Did they get stolen? Probably not, but regardless of their fate, I did not have these books to sell.

I had a near miss on my second visit to Houston when a box of books split open from the not so gentle handling by the USPS. Fortunately, the books did not get separated from the addressee's name and the USPS managed to still deliver them otherwise undamaged. So, I suspect that perhaps the earlier missing box of books in Mississippi might have had a similar fate, except that the P. O. couldn't figure out where to send them. After the Houston near miss, I started using more packing tape around the perimeter of the shipping boxes and using smaller and sturdier boxes.

Then there is the case of the phantom box of books I shipped in time for one of my San Francisco library talks, but which never got delivered by the P. O. Luckily, I discovered this problem before I left home for San Francisco and managed to bring a replacement box of books on the plane. The following week I discovered that the box was still sitting in the San Francisco branch post office! The P.O. claimed they tried to deliver them once but that no one was at the library to receive them. This explanation seemed rather suspicious, especially since they left no notice at the library of this attempt. By the time I learned the books were still at the P. O., I had already left San Francisco so my books and I were 400 miles apart. Fortunately, I asked relatives in town to retrieve and hold them for me since I was coming back in a few months to give another talk in San Francisco.

Whether the printer will deliver your books in time for your book talk is always a source of anxiety. There are few things worse than not having your book arrive until *after* your talk other than a shipment that *never* arrives, such as the box of books lost in Mississippi or the one that the San Francisco post office failed to deliver.

These problems do not exist for well-known authors with publishers that make arrangements with a local bookstore to handle book orders and sales. They bring and sell the books as well as handle the accounting. But authors generally have to give a hefty percentage of the sales to the bookstore, around 55 percent generally. As an independent small publisher, with inexpensive books to sell and travel costs to bear, there really is no way I could afford those costs.

One solution I stumbled upon after I published my second book was to use the services of a local printer with shorter turnaround times as well as lower prices than Lulu.com. I had somehow assumed that once I had Lulu.com print my books, I could not use a different printer. But once I discovered I was free to use other printers since I owned the rights to all my files, I searched for a local printer.

When I found a local printer in Anaheim, I went to discuss details for producing my books. Someone entered the office and after staring at me asked if I was not Mr. Jung. I did not recognize him so I asked how he knew me and I was startled and somewhat bemused when he told me that as an young adolescent he used to come to my house to play "Dungeons and Dragons" with my son, Jeff. It turned out that he was now the owner of this printing company and would become my printer for several years until I later decided to move to CreateSpace.com which had the advantages of Web resources for marketing. It not only could print paper versions of my books but also produce e-books.

There is both a plus and a minus to having four published books. People who come to hear a talk on one of my books may also find they have interest in some of my other titles, so I always bring copies of all four titles. But that also means I have to bring a greater total of books, which can be expensive to ship, and then have the burden of taking the unsold copies home.

At one talk I hit upon the idea of offering a discount on additional titles for anyone who wanted to buy more than one title. This simple tactic was very effective. Few people bought only one title, and quite a few purchased all four titles. They simply could not resist getting a discount on buying additional titles.

Getting to the talk venue can also be hair-raising. A friend, whose name will not be mentioned to avoid embarrassing him or her, drove me to one event. With about 10 minutes to spare, the friend realized that we were headed to the wrong restaurant and had to make an abrupt U-turn and speed to get to the actual site just in the nick of time. When driving to San Diego for a talk, I allowed myself three hours for the drive, which based on past trips to give talks there, takes about two hours. However, on this particular date, weekend bumper-to-bumper traffic clogged the freeway for miles. We phoned ahead to say we would be late, but fortunately, traffic congestion suddenly cleared and we managed to get there only five minutes late.

Arriving at the correct venue on time doesn't mean you are home free yet. In Hanford, California, for some unknown reason, I could not get the cable from my laptop to plug into the projector. After 10 or more minutes of frustration, I decided to just forego showing any slides and proceed. During the talk, which actually was going pretty smoothly, one of the staff members was kneeling in front of the podium trying to connect other cables to the computer while I spoke. We never got it connected, but the talk was still a success. After that talk, I stopped bringing my laptop and relied on the venue providing the equipment.

One other near disaster occurred during my second visit to Portland in 2013. Someone forgot to unlock the cabinet under the podium to provide access to the laptop. Security came but they did not have the right key. I resigned myself to just giving the talk without any slide presentation. At the last minute, someone found a staff person who knew where the right key was and we dodged another bullet.

O.K., can you relax once you have arrived at the correct place on time and the computer equipment is up and running? No, because once I found that the computer could not "read" my power point file off my zip drive, which was formatted for a Macintosh and could not be read by a PC. Fortunately, I had brought an extra zip drive for unforeseen problems such as this one. This other zip drive just happened, fortunately, to be PC formatted.

After that experience, I learned to arrange to send my power point file electronically a few days in advance to the venue and ask that it be preloaded and tested before the day of the talk. This procedure also saves precious time as I have often seen speakers lose many minutes of speaking time while problems loading files are solved. Murphy's Law, "If anything can go wrong, it will," holds true much too often!

How to fund travel to give talks

The story behind each event is somewhat different, with invitations for some events being a matter of dumb luck, others arranged through "connections," and some set up through my initiative and persuasion. For some events at distant sites, I have been fortunate to receive funds for travel and lodging. Where only airfare was offered, I accepted the opportunity if I could get free lodging with hosts, friends, or relatives.

Using a "piggy-back" strategy, I try to combine business with pleasure. For example, I arranged for my New York talk to be on the day after I attended a 90th birthday party for a relative. I saved costs by arranging to do two or three talks at a given city to different groups within a day or two. In a few instances, I was willing to bear all the costs of my travel and lodging because that venue was in a part of the country where I had not previously spoken and I wanted to be regarded as someone who spoke "from coast-to-coast." More important to me than making a profit from my "career" in Chinese American history was spreading the word about the contents of my books, which I felt more Americans, Chinese as well as non-Chinese, needed to know. Fortunately, my talks have generally been very well received and I have been able to sell enough books to offset most of my travel expenses.

As an independent (someone with a shoe-string budget) author/publisher, I have no funds from a publisher for travel to book signing events that a well-recognized author might have for a book published by a major company. I would have to pay for any advertising and promotional publicity. Either I only give local talks where I do not have to incur lodging and air travel costs or I have to find ways to combine a talk and a visit to that area with personal business or recreation. Making such arrangements can be difficult. Advance planning is needed to coordinate the talk and any other purposes for travelling to that site. If I am fortunate to sell enough books, any profits can be used to offset or cover my travel expenses.

I like to imagine that some day any organization that would really want me to come speak would find ways to fund my travel costs. Until that day, I try to be creative in financing my out-of-town travel. There have been a few instances where my hosts have come up with small honorariums or speaker fees to pay or at least offset my travel costs, and some universities have provided free housing during my visit. In some instances, someone with an extra room will provide housing and local transportation. And in the worst case, I generally get a nice complimentary meal at a nice restaurant in the company of some interested audience members after the talk.

Importance of shameless self-promotion

It may be difficult to believe after reading accounts of my many acts of shameless self-promotion about my foray into writing on Chinese American history that I am actually a rather modest person who, while not suffering from stage fright, is usually reticent to speak in public. However, I learned very early on that with self-publishing, it was essential for any hope of success to take advantage of every opportunity to speak to audiences. I had to publicize and promote my books by sharing any compliments and endorsements that readers, audience members, book reviewers, and academic scholars offered.

Marketing and promotion of books call for a different mindset than what is involved in researching and writing. It also consumes valuable time and energy that could be used for writing. But without devoting efforts to speaking at book signings, posting on social media, and writing interesting blogs, your books, no matter how worthwhile, may go unnoticed.

Endnotes

[1] Questions of Chinese-black sexual relations in the Mississippi Delta and throughout the South were a sensitive topic. In the days of Chinese exclusion when there were very few Chinese women allowed to enter the country, some Chinese men sought interracial sexual or marital arrangements. Social norms and customs disapproved of Chinese men having such relations with white women, but ignored them between Chinese men and black women. However, in Chinese communities, mixed relationships, especially with blacks, were frowned upon because they jeopardized acceptance of Chinese by white society.

[2] A sample of websites useful for self-publishing. http://kwout.com/t/f4jqs3aq

12. Some Closing Thoughts

My fortune cookie read: Prepare to meet the unexpected.

My journey of discovery of personal history and the Chinese American past has been remarkable in many exciting and unexpected ways. The many coincidences and linkages among experiences I have had and the people I have met are more incredible than anything I could have made up.

Meeting Madame Chiang Kai-shek in Macon in 1943

In Chapter 1, I mentioned the visit of Madame Chiang Kai-shek to Macon in 1943 when I was only 6 years old. I still vividly recall that day as it was a typical hot and humid June afternoon when my three siblings and I, the only Chinese children in town, somehow found ourselves standing in the broiling sun amid an overflow crowd waiting for what seemed to be forever to catch a glimpse of Madame Chiang Kai-shek, easily the Jacqueline Kennedy of her day, at the ceremony honoring her at the Wesleyan College Conservatory in Macon.

Being only 6 years old at the time (I am circled in the picture below), I did not know who this celebrity was, why she was in Macon, and most importantly, why I had to be there! The local newspaper coverage shown below was extensive, gushing with pride that this most influential woman in China, and possibly, along with Eleanor Roosevelt, in the world, was in Macon.

Although I was too young to know how important this woman was, the journalist wrote that it was "a big day for the four tiny Jungs," eager to see "their heroine." This event occurred during the historic visit of Madame Chiang to the United States to rally support for China's struggle against the Japanese invasion. She addressed Congress and visited major Chinatowns across the country to raise financial support for China, and it is thought that her presence had considerable influence on the repeal of the 1882 Chinese Exclusion Act in 1943.

Macon newspaper coverage of Madame Chiang Kai-shek' visit, 1943.

It would not be until half a century later that I discovered, with the aid of a local archivist, that when Madame Chiang Kai-shek was a young girl, she not only lived in Macon with her two older sisters for several years, but in 1910, she was denied admission to a local elementary school because she was "an alien." (See the clipping pasted at the lower right corner of the image of the newspaper page). And, a generation later, she was welcomed as an ally of the U. S. in World War II. Such are the often strange twists of history!

In hindsight, I have to ask myself whether this brush with Madame Chiang in some mysterious manner influenced my eventual fascination with the history of Chinese in America that developed over half a century later. My memory tells me that we never actually got to meet Madame Chiang and probably never got within 100 yards of her. My sister Jean more or less confirmed my suspicion that we were just brought in as window dressing, just in case Madame Chiang asked if there were any Chinese in town!

Constructing accurate Chinese family histories

The primary information for tracing family histories generally comes from what parents, older siblings, aunts, uncles, grandparents, and other older relatives tell us about the family relationships, events, and experiences. Unfortunately, however, due to misremembered details, suppressed as well as embellished accounts, and forgetting, family histories can be highly inaccurate. Information about the family's past from outside sources such as acquaintances and friends allows some crosschecking. Even here, however, if there is disagreement among sources, how does one determine which account is valid?

Official records - birth, marriage, and death records - could be helpful sources for corroborating the retrospective recall of relatives. Archival records, such as transcripts of immigration records, might be useful, except that many Chinese used false identity papers during the years of the Chinese Exclusion Act (1882-1943). Moreover, the testimony in these files, assuming one can even locate them, is invalid for determining true family relationships for immigrants with false identity documents who entered as paper sons. Family relationships in their testimony applied to the family of the person whose papers they had acquired, not to their own family.

Locating the immigration file for a Chinese immigrant can prove difficult for many reasons, including looking in the wrong archive. Consider the case of one immigrant that I know about. He first entered the United States at San Francisco. On several subsequent trips to China, he sometimes re-entered at Seattle and other times at San Francisco. The daughter searched in vain for his immigration file because she was confused about the port of his *original* entry. She had been looking for his file in the wrong place, Seattle, but I helped her find his file by directing her to the archive for the port of his original entry, San Francisco.

Knowing the names of immigrants, true or false, may not be sufficient for finding their files. Immigration officers and census takers sometimes recorded Chinese names incorrectly because they were not familiar with Chinese names. They sometimes reversed the order of their given and surnames because Chinese names start with the surname first, unlike American names. Illegible handwriting by census enumerators might lead to errors in transferring them to databases For example, in one immigrant's file, the father's first name was recorded as "Quikzip," which was an unlikely name. I was able to check with a descendant who informed me that his real name was "Tuck Yip."

I found complicated situations that illustrate why it is so difficult to determine family histories for Chinese immigrants. For example, when immigrants came as paper sons using false papers, siblings of the same parents could end up with different surnames. I know one family where each of the three sons entered using different surnames.

In another complicated case, parents arrived with several young children but the children were carefully coached to refer to their mother as their aunt in the presence of immigration officials. Their mother had to pose as a sister rather than as the wife of her husband so that her identity corresponded with the false identity papers she was using to gain entry.

Another immigrant benefited from the unfortunate death of the son of another family in his village. The purchased identity papers of the deceased boy enabled another man's son of about the same age to gain admission to the United States.

Another story involved the switching of identities between the same aged sons of two distant relatives. The son of one man came to the U. S. using the papers of his uncle's Number 2 son. A few years later, when the uncle brought his Number 2 son over, he no longer had his son's own papers and he had to use the papers of the Number 3 son who came over three years later (but no mention was made of how he got papers).

Other complications could arise when some men had children by different wives or when some families adopted children, usually boys, by families that had no sons of their own.

When we want to know the past, it is often too late

I have received occasional requests from Chinese who have seen some of my works and thought that perhaps I might be able to help in their quest to find out information about their ancestors who came from China to United States over a century ago. Although I felt flattered that they thought I had such skills, unfortunately I was unable, with a few exceptions, to find the information about the ancestors.

A second-generation Chinese American emailed me in 2013 for help in locating her father. She said that her paternal great-grandfather came from China in the late 1870s and lived on the West Coast. His two sons, one the grandfather of my respondent, came over later in 1883 and lived for a few years with their father. One of them, her father, moved to Greenville, Mississippi in 1888 where he opened a grocery store. He moved around frequently, going first to Clarksdale, Mississippi, and then Austin, Texas. After a trip back to China, he returned to work in New York and Baltimore. Then he moved back to the South, first to Memphis and then to Shelby and Canton in the Mississippi Delta before finally settling in Seattle.

My respondent admitted that when she was growing up she never thought to ask her father about his childhood and aside from knowing his birthplace, she had little knowledge about his past. Her father passed away before she took an active interest in finding out more about his past. About a decade ago she searched library archives for genealogy information. A few limited findings piqued her interest but the trail got cold and she put aside the research. As her children grew up, she wanted to present more of their family history to them. She even established contact with some cousins in China who shared the same grandfather. Recently she resumed online searches, entering some names and places that were relevant, and was surprised to find something I had written about Chinese in Mississippi that caught her attention.

> "Something you have written matched something I read in my grandfather's files. The grocery store my grandfather owned was burned down in 1914. The name of his partner who helped watch the store for him while he traveled to/from China was similar to "Fung Lee" or maybe "Fong Lee." At least that was the name of the store. I hope you can help me find out whether there was such a store and whether they know anything about the burned-out store. The trail is getting warmer again."

Unfortunately, my searches for additional information online and from my Delta Chinese friends did not turn up anything else of value about her family history. Nonetheless, it was gratifying to learn that she found my information somewhat helpful.

Preaching beyond the choir

It has been rewarding to speak to interested audiences across the country about my books on aspects of the history of Chinese in America. The majority of my audiences, however, have consisted of Chinese Americans, mostly immigrants and their descendants born here as well as overseas. Audiences usually had older Chinese, ones likely to have had direct experience with the limited opportunities and mistreatment of Chinese in the past. In effect, I was "preaching to the choir" because as noted earlier, I was not telling most of these audiences anything they did not already know.

But how do I attract audiences of non-Chinese, young as well as old, who might find it worthwhile to learn about this history? I have already described my several opportunities to widen my audiences through talks at several meetings of some of the chapters of the U.S.-China Peoples Friendship Association, whose membership consists mostly of non-Chinese "Sinophiles" who have an extensive knowledge of China.

In 2011 I had the opportunity to speak at California State University, Long Beach where I had taught Psychology for 40 years. In my talk, I described how I "reinvented myself" after retiring to become a "public historian" of Chinese American immigrant businesses. Since I was speaking to psychology students rather than to my usual audience of mostly Chinese people, I focused on explaining how my newfound retirement career developed as I wrote my books and gave book talks across the country, instead of discussing in any detail the content of my books on Chinese American history.

To generate strong interest, I shared some of the more improbable unexpected events that occurred. I emphasized how important it was to develop connections and networks, and to take risks by accepting new challenges. Hopefully, they learned that retirement is a state of mind to a large extent, and that one must be open to new opportunities and experiences.

Psychology Department talk, California State University, Long Beach, 2011.

Who needs to know the history of Chinese in America?

Learning about the history of how Chinese came to North America and how they were so terribly mistreated prompted me to actively educate others, non-Chinese as well as Chinese, about the past. Some might argue that history is the past, and we should let bygones be bygones. In some respects, this is a useful attitude, as lamenting past injustices can be an exercise in unproductive anger and resentment. On the other hand, there are lessons from history that we need to learn. As philosopher George Santayana observed, "Those who cannot remember the past are condemned to repeat it."

Some also hold that there is less need to recall past injustices inflicted on Chinese because of the great reduction in racial intolerance over the past generation. Nonetheless, aftereffects of past attitudes and stereotypes still linger. History cannot be fully erased or deleted the way one can reformat a computer disk drive. Chinese, and other Asian Americans, are still seen by some as "forever foreign," a long-standing attitude from the past that refuses to die and occasionally rises anew.

As William Faulkner famously wrote, "The past is never dead. It's not even past." Knowledge of the awful past is important, not only for descendents of the generations of Chinese who suffered oppressive racism, but also for descendants of those who were their oppressors. Only when all parties begin to recognize, regret, and reform racist attitudes and practices can any real progress occur toward establishing and maintaining a more equitable society.

The many faces of Chinese in America

Before the 1950s, Chinese in America consisted of a relatively homogenous group, mainly poor immigrants from rural villages in Guangdong province in southern China. They came to seek gold, but many wound up building railroads, farming, and working in laundries and restaurants. They and their descendants, born here and in China, were the primary source of Chinese in America for several decades. Many had a family history of "paper sons" or false identities among earlier family members who immigrated during the years of the Chinese Exclusion laws, and this past continues to exert a burden on the descendants.

In contrast, as pointed out in Chapter 6, in the mid 1960s, Chinese began coming here from many places in Asia other than Guangdong. Unlike the earlier Guangdong immigrants, many of these later Chinese immigrants were highly educated, often with professional and scientific skills, substantial financial assets, and some proficiency in English. And, they spoke Mandarin whereas the earlier cohorts of Guangdong immigrants spoke Cantonese or Toishan-wa.

Not all newer Chinese immigrants, however, were well off. There were also poorer Chinese from Fujian province next to Guangdong, who had to work long hours for low wages over many years to pay off their debts incurred to smugglers for enabling their illegal entry.

It is important to recognize that many newer Chinese immigrants do not seek to assimilate to or adopt Western customs, at least not to the extent that earlier generations did. Indeed, many of these Chinese are transnational in outlook, with one foot here while keeping the other foot in their country of origin. Unlike the descendants of the earliest waves of Guangdong Chinese with historical ties to gold mining, railroad construction, laundry and restaurant work in North America, the newer Chinese have links to a different history, that of their own homeland.

Thus, the history of Taiwan immigrants and their descendants is tied to the flight from China to Taiwan after the Communist regime took over in 1949, the history of Hong Kong Chinese immigrants and their descendents is based on the British rule that lasted until 1997, and the history of mainland Chinese immigrants is linked to the rule of the Communist regime since 1949. Finally, whereas the earlier Guangdong immigrants were never more than a small minority in America, more recent Chinese are coming to a United States that has a rapidly growing population of Asian immigrants.

The significance of this changing composition of more recent Chinese immigrants is that they are unlikely to feel that the earlier history of Chinese in America is relevant for them. In one sense, they are correct, but in a broader sense, they are mistaken. In the view of many non-Chinese Americans, subgroups of Chinese are indistinguishable despite their different histories and places of origin. Irrespective of where they came from, how long they have been here, their level of education, or their degree of assimilation, in the eyes of many non-Chinese, Chinese all "look the same," so they will be prone to treat all Chinese the same way.

Let me make a point with an anecdote. A student from Taiwan told me following a talk that while it was interesting to learn about the prejudices against Chinese from Guangdong from the late 1860s well into the following century, he wondered, "I come from Taiwan. What does this history have to do with me?"

At first I was taken aback by his somewhat blunt query, but one that I did not perceive to be hostile. He honestly did not find it relevant for his personal life. It took me a few seconds to decide what to say, but I replied,

> Let's imagine you and I are walking down Main Street together and some non-Chinese who happen to dislike foreigners, spot us. They are not going to say, or think, "Oh, there goes one Chinese from Taiwan and one with roots from Guangdong." No, they are more likely to say, "There goes two Chinks (or Chinamen)."

> If you knew the history of how Chinese were mistreated in America for decades, you would not be at all surprised by this comment or how they might behave badly toward us, but if you are ignorant of this history, you would be shocked or at least confused. That is why even if your roots are not in Guangdong, as a Chinese you need to know the history of Chinese in America because that past still has a potential adverse impact on how you, and all other Chinese, will be treated.

The negative images of Chinese and the prejudices against them in the past have definitely lessened over recent decades, but are dormant and can resurface at any moment. Improvements in the status of Chinese in America from the end of World War II until recent times may lead to complacency. However, in the decade of the 2010s, China is increasingly portrayed again as the "yellow peril," a view with negative spillover effects because many non-Chinese may make the mistake of seeing Chinese in America as similar, if not equivalent, to Chinese in China. It is dangerous for Chinese in America to *not* know this history.

Why have I become more Chinese as I get older?

As I noted earlier, growing up in Macon, with no contact with a Chinese community or peers, my social interactions were by necessity with either black or white people. As I was neither black nor white, I was always more or less an outsider. Under these conditions, race or ethnicity was an issue that I tried to avoid thinking about.

Announcement for my talk at Arizona State University, 2006.

Even after moving to San Francisco at age 15, and coming in constant contact with scores of Chinese Americans of my own age as well as with the larger Chinese community, ethnicity was still not a primary concern for me. Only after I started writing *Southern Fried Rice* did my inner Chinese begin to awaken. The more I dug into the history of Chinese in America, the more interested I became in learning more and I began to write and speak on this history. Seeing the keen interest in my findings among my readers and audiences further energized my efforts that led me to create several websites that enabled me to continue to supplement and add material to the content of my books.

In my preface, I expressed hope that my efforts might guide and encourage others to undertake similar writing, so I was delighted to find a reader of *Sweet and Sour* wrote on her blog,[1]

> "...Just reading his Life After Retirement bio, I realize how similar our Chinese-American/Canadian paths have been. He grew up a "laundry kid" in Macon, Georgia where his family was the only Chinese in town (I grew up in Halifax, Nova Scotia, on the eastern end of Canada) and then he moved to San Francisco where there are plenty of Chinese but he still didn't fit in with San Francisco Chinese who lived with so many Chinese all their lives (ditto, I moved to "Hongcouver"/Vancouver, British Columbia). I love how John Jung has the ability to pursue his interest during his retirement and I hope to do that as well."

My own sense of being Chinese has undergone a substantial transformation during this journey. I now have a stronger "Chinese" identity than I ever had previously. It is the knowledge that I acquired from studying the historical evidence about how Chinese were victimized in America and how Chinese were able to still achieve success and contribute positively to society that helped me recognize, accept, and celebrate the Chinese side of my Chinese American identity.

Endnotes

[1] http://www.catchstargirl.com/?p=1917

Epilog: Macon Revisited

When I returned to my hometown of Macon as an invited speaker at the 2006 Georgia Literary Festival. I had some startling experiences in seeing, or not seeing, some of the old landmarks in the town.

Whittle School, my elementary school, had received a facelift with a modernized façade but was now an office complex. The Ritz Theatre where I spent many a happy Saturday afternoon enjoying a double feature of B-grade cowboy movies, Three Stooges comedies, and serialized episodes of Dick Tracy, Superman, and others was no longer there.

In contrast, the only theatre where "coloreds" could view movies, the Douglass Theatre (no relation to Frederick Douglass), had been totally refurbished and was a beautiful venue for stage events.

Did the Confederate soldier statue get moved, and why?

One of the most surprising experiences of my first visit back to Macon, in 2004, was seeing the old Confederate soldier statue that I recall passing every day on my way to and from Whittle School had apparently marched on to a new site. It had stood, since 1896 or thereabouts, atop a small mound of grass "smack dab," as locals would say, in the center of the intersection of my street, Mulberry, and Second Street, only a block away from one of the main streets of Macon.

But in 2004, the statue was *not* where I remembered it. Instead, it stood on a nearby triangular plot of land where Second St. collided with a diagonal street, Cotton Ave. only about 50 to 75 feet away from its original site.

Still it seemed to fit there so well in this location that I began to wonder if my memory could have failed so badly. Looking at the middle of the intersection of Mulberry and Second Streets where I believed the statue used to be located, I saw that in its place, left turn lanes had been installed to permit cars on Second St. to more readily make left turns onto Mulberry Street. Follow the arrows in the diagram below to see where the statue had been and where it was relocated.

Confederate Monument.
Second and Mulberry Streets,
Macon, Ga.

Confederate Soldier monument was a block from our laundry.

Aha, now it all made sense. When "push came to shove," the modern need to keep traffic moving triumphed over the sanctity of monuments to the past. Our Confederate soldier had to yield to the convenience of motorists!

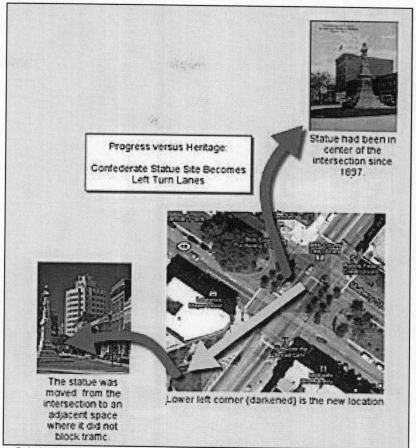

Original and new sites of Confederate soldier statue on Mulberry Street.

In 2011, I came to Macon again. I had been invited to give a talk at the Crossroads Writers Literary Festival. My host and best friend from grammar school, Richard Harris, took me one afternoon to a lunch reunion with a few of the guys I had gone to junior high school with. When we entered the City Grill Restaurant on the corner of Third and Cherry Streets, I had a sense of déjà vu and finally realized that this restaurant occupied what was the J. J. Newberry 5 and 10 cent store when I was growing up in Macon. I used to spent time, and a little money, buying toys from the toy section in the basement.

Did they move the Third Street fountain and pool?

During lunch, I glanced out the restaurant window and noticed a water fountain in the middle of a circular pool with a diameter of about 15 feet in the median park on Third Street near Cherry Street. It definitely looked familiar, but I sensed that it was not located where I remembered it being during my childhood. I used to make paper boats to see how far they would float across the pond on a summer afternoon. I could have sworn that the fountain and pool had been on the other side of Cherry Street across from the Dempsey Hotel than where it currently was but Richard assured me that it had always been in its present site.

I found I had an old picture postcard that confirmed my memory was correct. It shows where the fountain and pool was located in the 1940s, which was not where I found it in 2011.

Location of the Third Street fountain when I lived in Macon.

The legendary Rip Van Winkle returned to his hometown after a 20-year slumber, and he was astounded by the changes that had occurred during his absence. Imagine then how much more change I saw in Macon after an absence of around half a century. Yet, many of the physical features of Macon were still the same at least on the surface. Public buildings such as City Hall, the courthouse, the train station, and the post office still looked much the same although they had been repurposed in some instances.

The train station, a beautiful classic federal style building that once was my doorway for occasional visits to the larger world of Atlanta, was now relegated to serve as an information headquarters for visitors, who ironically arrived mostly by automobile.

It was an emotional and in some ways, surreal, experience to walk around the downtown area, which was in decay in many sections, and to recall what it had been like when I was growing up.

The writing of *Southern Fried* Rice gave me two opportunities to give talks about the book in Macon, the "stage" where its story about our family unfolded so many years ago and remains an indelible part of me. It was an emotional experience in which a hometown boy gets to return to his birthplace and share his memories with local residents.

Standing in front of Sam Lee Laundry site during a visit in 2004.

But the biggest shock I experienced in my several return visits to Macon was in 2004 when I took my wife, Phyllis, to show her the site of our family's laundry. To my surprise and dismay, the building on Mulberry Street that had housed the Sam Lee Laundry since 1885, and where my family worked and lived from 1928 to 1956, had been razed and replaced with a paved metered parking lot. The building had never been anything more than a modest structure, but it had been home to our family. The realization that it had been replaced with a parking lot felt insulting.

In retrospect, I believe that was the very moment when I resolved to write *Southern Fried Rice*. Seeing that the laundry building no longer existed physically, to me it was as if we had never existed there either. I felt a duty to write our story as a testament that our Chinese laundry and family had been a part of Macon's history.

Yes, it had been quite a shock to see that the building in which we lived and worked as the only Chinese family in Macon during the Jim Crow era in the Deep South… was "gone with the wind."

On another visit a few years later, I discovered that the entire side of Mulberry Street in the heart of downtown Macon where our laundry had been located was gone and replaced with new structures. The asphalt parking lot that occupied the site of our laundry when I visited Macon in 2004 was now the site of an enclosed brick parking structure, which I suppose could be considered an upgrade of sorts. Over the course of a century, the face of the side of the 500 block of Mulberry Street that I grew up on changed drastically, but my prejudiced view is that it has not been for the better.

Sam Lee Laundry (est. 1885) Mulberry Street site in 1906, 1953, 2011.

Bibliography

Bao, Xiaolan. *Holding Up More than Half The Sky: Chinese Women Garment Workers in New York City, 1948-92*. Urbana, IL.: University of Illinois Press, 2006.

Bragg, Walter. "Not A Chinese in Our Town For First Time in A Century." *Macon News*, March 6, 1956, 4.

Healey, Patrick J. and Chew, Ng Poon. "A statement for non-exclusion." San Francisco. (1905).

Jung, John. "Gong Lum v. Rice 1927: Mississippi School Segregation and the Delta Chinese." *Chinese American Forum*, 2011, Volume XXVI (3) 21-24.

Jung, John. "The Sour Side of Chinese Restaurants," *Chinese American Forum*, 2013,XXIX (1), 1-22.

Loewen, James W. *The Mississippi Chinese. Between Black and White*. Second Ed. Prospect Heights, IL.: Waveland Press, 1988.

Quan, Robert Seto. *Lotus Among the Magnolias: The Mississippi Chinese*. Jackson: The University of Mississippi Press, 1982.

Siu, Paul C. P. *The Chinese Laundryman: A Study of Social Isolation*. New York: New York University Press, 1987.

Seligman, Scott D. *Three Tough Chinamen*. Hong Kong: Earnshaw Books, Ltd., 2012.

Stockwell, Foster. "An Unknown Chapter in Chinese American History." *Chinese American Forum*, 2010, 26, 2, 35-36.

Sue, Sam. "Growing up in Mississippi." *Asian Americans. Oral Histories of First to Fourth Generation Americans from China, the Philippines, Japan. India, the Pacific Islands. Vietnam and Cambodia*. edited by Joann Faung and Jean Lee (New York: The New Press. 1991) 3-9.

Young, Grace. *The Wisdom of the Chinese Kitchen*. New York: Simon and Shuster, 1999.

Yung, Judy. *The Adventures of Eddie Fung: Chinatown Kid, Texas Cowboy, Prisoner of War*. Seattle: University of Washington Press, 2011.

Appendix: Book Talk Venues

Historical Museums
Chinese Historical Society of America, San Francisco, 2006, 2014
Museum of Chinese in America, New York, 2006
San Diego Chinese History Museum, San Diego, 2007, 2009, 2010
Chinese Historical Society of Southern California, 2007, 2010, 2011
Chinese American Museum of Chicago, 2008, 2011
Chinese American Museum of Northern California, Marysville, California. 2008
Locke Historical Dedication Event, Locke, California. 2008

Chinese Organizations & Events
Organization of Chinese Americans, Atlanta 2007
Who's Who in Asian American Communities in Georgia, Atlanta 2007
Chinese Consolidated Benevolent Society, Augusta, Georgia. 2007
Chinese American Citizen's Alliance, Salinas, California, 2008
Chinese American Citizen's Alliance, Leland, Mississippi, 2008
National Assn. of Asian American Professionals, Atlanta, 2007
Chinese Professional Club, Houston, Texas, 2008, 2009
Chinese Cultural Society of Stockton, California, 2008
Sacramento Chinese Cultural Foundation, 2008
Marin Chinese Cultural Association, San Rafael, California. 2008
Foo's Ho Ho Restaurant Fundraiser, Vancouver, Canada, 2010
Chinese American Historical Societies Conference, Seattle, 2013
Portland Chinese Scholarship Foundation, 2012, 2013
Portland Chinese High School Graduation Dinner, 2013
Chinese Historical Society of New England, Boston, 2013
Asian Pacific American Historical Society, Atlanta, 2010, 2014
Mississippi Delta Chinese Heritage Museum Reunion, 2014

Colleges & Universities
Occidental College, Los Angeles, 2006
California State University, Long Beach, Psychology, 2011

California State University, Long Beach Asian American Studies classes, 2011-2013
California State University, Long Beach, Liberal Arts Emeriti, 2009
California State University, Long Beach Emeriti, 2011
California State University, Fullerton Asian American Studies, 2008
Downtown City College of San Francisco, 2014
Emory University, Atlanta, 2011
Mercer University, Educational Psychology, Macon, Georgia. 2007
Arizona State University, Asian American Studies. 2008
Delta State University, Cleveland, Mississippi, 2008, 2011
Jackson State University, Jackson, Mississippi, 2008
University of Memphis, 2011
University of Memphis Campus School 5th Grade, 2011
University of Mississippi, Oxford, Mississippi, 2011
Bridgewater State University, Bridgewater, Massachusetts, 2013

Libraries
Carnegie Library, Clarksdale, Mississippi, 2008
Hanford Public Library, Hanford, California, 2007
Heritage Park Regional Library, Irvine, California, 2010
Foster City Public Library, Foster City, California, 2008, 2011, 2012
Cerritos Public Library, California, 2009, 2010
Alhambra Public Library, Alhambra, California, 2010
San Francisco Chinatown Library, 2010
San Francisco Main Library, 2010
Long Beach Library, 2012
Monterey Park Library, 2011, 2012
Signal Hill Library, California, 2011
Torrance Library, California, 2012, 2013
Rosemead Library, California, May, October, 2013

Other Organizations
Desert Jade Women's Club, Phoenix, Arizona. 2008
Chi-Am Circle Club, Cupertino, California, 2007, 2010
Association of Chinese Cooking Teachers, Alameda, California, 2010
Chateau Cupertino Senior Residence, 2010, 2011
Leisure Village, Camarillo, California, 2010

International Food Services Employees Assn. Pasadena, California, 2011
U.S. China Peoples Friendship Assn. Long Beach, 2011, 2014
U.S. China Peoples Friendship Assn. National Seminar. Washington, D. C., 2012
U.S. China Peoples Friendship Assn. Western Region Conference, San Gabriel, California, 2012
Seal Beach International Friendship Association, 2013
American Assn. of University Women, La Palma-Cerritos, 2013
Interview for Clothesline Muse documentary, Insibah Films, 2013
Asian American Club, The Villages, Orlando Florida, 2014

Churches
Berkeley Chinese Community Church, 2007, 2008, 2009, 2011
Community Christian Alliance Church, Northridge, California, 2008
Universalist Unitarian Church, Macon, Georgia, 2007

Literary Events
Writers Group, Lake Havasu City, Arizona. 2008
Georgia Literary Festival, Macon, Georgia, 2007
Culinary Historians of Northern California, San Francisco, 2011
Crossroads Writers & Literary Conference, Macon, Georgia, 2011
Festival of Authors, Duarte, California, 2013
East Wind Books, Berkeley, California, 2014

Radio-Television
Interview, *Bay Area People*, KTVU-TV, Oakland, California,. 2006
Chinese Laundry Kids, CBC Radio, Vancouver, Canada, 2010
WABE Interview on "One on One" Steve Goss, Atlanta, 2011
Mississippi Public Radio, Interview by Sandra Knispel 2011
KBOO-FM APA Compass Interview, Portland, Oregon 2012
Interview, CNC World Xinhua News TV, 2012
RTHK Hong Kong Television Documentary, 2012
Who's Talking, Interview on WCHL-FM, Chapel Hill, North Carolina, 2012
Chewing the Fat. Interview, WBEZ, Chicago, 2014.
Asian Pacific American Historical Society Google Hangout Book discussion, 2014.

Index

cultural isolation, 36

Wong, David, 147-148
Wong, Donna, 42
Wong, Ed, 78
Wong, Emma, 168
Wong, Flo Oy, 78, 85-86, 167
Wong, Frank, 151-152
Wong, Helen, 50, 59-60, 72
Wong, Henry, 61, 74-75
Wong, Jon, 106, 109
Wong, Julie Hornsby, 87, 167
Wong, Leland, 91, 147,
    two Leland Wongs, 149-152
Wong, Nellie, 61, 78, 86, 167
Wong, Paul, 59, 62, 106, 151
Wong, Raymond, 80
Wong, Rod, xiii, 42
World Journal, 168
Wu, P. C., 80

Xie, Elwin, 42, 96

Yau, Annie, 105-110, 118
Yee, Candy, 116
Yee, Hay, 151
Yee, Kelvin Han, 48
Yeh, Andrew, KBOO-FM, 108
Yeh, Claire, 114
Yick Wo v. Hopkins (1885), 44
Yin & Yang ex/Press/ions, 166-167
Yin and Yang Press, iii, 9, 92, 104,
    161, 164, 168-169, 171
Yon, Stanley, 131
York University, 4, 214
Young, Grace, 81, 88
Young, Joe, 59
YouTube, 21, 91, 162, 164
Yu, Henry, 178
Yuen, Mary, 115
Yung, Judy, xii, 15, 148

Zhang, Ambassador Yesui, 103-104
Zuckerman, JoRae, 159

Made in the USA
San Bernardino, CA
14 January 2015